INCOME REDISTRIBUTION
AND THE WELFARE STATE

ADRIAN L. WEBB

Lecturer in Social Administration
London School of Economics and Political Science

and

JACK E. B. SIEVE, Ph.D., F.C.A.

OCCASIONAL PAPERS ON SOCIAL ADMINISTRATION NO. 41
*Editorial Committee under the
Chairmanship of Professor R. M. Titmuss*

*Published by G. Bell & Sons,
York House, Portugal Street, London, W.C.2*

First published 1971

© *1971 by The Social Administration Research Trust*

ISBN 0 7135 1806 5

MADE AND PRINTED IN ENGLAND BY
WILLMER BROTHERS LIMITED
BIRKENHEAD

FOREWORD

This series of *Occasional Papers* was started in 1960 to supply the need for a medium of publication for studies in the field of social policy and administration which fell between the two extremes of the short article and the full-length book. It was thought that such a series would not only meet a need among research workers and writers concerned with contemporary social issues, but would also strengthen links between students of the subject and administrators, social workers, committee members and others with responsibilities and interest in the social services.

Many of the papers in this series have been written by members of the Department of Social Science and Administration at the London School of Economics and Political Science. Contributions are, however, welcome from workers in other universities and institutions and should be submitted to the Editorial Committee. A list of most of earlier papers which are still in print is printed on the back of this volume.

Richard M. Titmuss

CONTENTS

This study owes much to the original work on income distribution published by Richard Titmuss, our debt will be apparent to all who are acquainted with his research. In addition, however, we are greatly indebted to him and to Brian Abel-Smith for encouragement, advice and criticism.

Many others have offered valuable comments and we would particularly thank Howard Glennerster, Sally Sainsbury and members of the Central Statistical Office for their very useful criticisms of various drafts.

We are indebted to a number of people for typing successive drafts, but our largest debts are to Anne Edwards and Helen Burns for their very considerable and patient help.

Responsibility for the deficiencies of the study remains with us of course, but without the help received the defects would have been far more numerous.

1. EGALITARIAN POLICIES AND THE 'WELFARE STATE'

Publicly financed social services are the major means of providing for a wide range of social needs in our society. In largely replacing the market as a method of allocating a range of goods and services they presumably give rise to a distribution of resources which the market mechanism would not have produced. However, the redistribution of resources that the social services should produce, or are intended to produce, cannot easily be specified. Expectations about the past and present impact of social welfare provision on our society are difficult to state in a precise form. Since many groups and individuals participate in the formation of social policies, as many expectations exist concerning the distribution of resources that should result from the social policies that are enacted. The collectivity of social services now in existence and the processes by which each has developed into its present form, are not characterized by a homogeneity of objectives. We cannot expect there to be a consensus of opinion on the pursuit of any given level of income redistribution through the social services.

Nevertheless, this complexity at the level of intent does not prevent us asking a basic factual question. Do the social services in practice produce a redistribution of resources in our society? Whether one considers the social services per se, or any one of them in particular, this must be one of the most fundamental questions against which to assess the way in which they operate. For many people the concept of redistribution immediately suggests movements of resources from the richer to the poorer members of the society and the 'welfare state' is widely believed to be redistributive in this sense. Studies exist which throw some light on this basic issue and this book is devoted to an examination of these studies, in order to determine how far they are able to answer the question we have just posed.

Accordingly, ours is a study of the methodology used in quantifying the redistribution effected by social policies and it is an attempt to explore the complexity of the problems facing researchers in this field of inquiry. Three major research projects have been conducted in our area of interest, by Barna (relating to 1937), Cartter (relating to 1948/49), and Nicholson (relating to various years from 1953 to the present).[1] The studies by Barna and Cartter are discussed briefly (mainly in Appendix I but also in Chapter Two) to indicate the innovations in research methods that have occurred in recent years. The methodology of Nicholson's research is then considered in detail in Chapters Three, Four and Five. To produce data on income redistribution which are directly relevant to the discussions of social policy, is not at all easy. We have indicated the major difficulties which have to be overcome during the course of our discussion of Nicholson's research.

We include some calculations of our own in Chapter Five. These are primarily intended to emphasize aspects of the methodological problems discussed and they do not amount to a comprehensive estimate of redistribution. The final chapter summarizes the data which have become available through Nicholson's work and presents some tentative conclusions about the nature and level of income redistribution effected through the social services.

Before proceeding to discuss specific studies of redistribution, however, it is important to indicate in a general way the confusion which has surrounded some of the concepts that we will be employing. Due to their complexity, redistribution studies consume substantial research effort and require justification. Their value does not lie merely in the exploration of a crucial facet of the social structure of our society and the monitoring of change (if any) in the distribution of real income. They are also important because of the misconceptions which have developed about the intended and actual role of social welfare policies in promoting greater social equality and the light they may shed on this subject.

The Egalitarian Connotations of 'The Welfare State'.

The diversity of intentions and objectives invested in social policies was stressed in the first paragraph of this chapter. But the complexity of social policy does not prevent the emergence of misleadingly simple views about the impact of such policies. When social welfare programmes are aggregated and referred to as a collectivity it is particularly easy to ignore their heterogeneity and ascribe objectives, roles and achievements to the collectivity. This process is legitimate in an attempt to inject meaning into an untidy agglomeration of historical phenomena. It is also legitimate in characterizing the mood and intentions of important participants in, or contemporary observers, of, a period of intensive policy formation. However, the same collective expressions, ('the social services', 'the welfare state', 'social policy') that are used in such exercises are also used in evaluating our present policies and in discussing future developments. Public and political debate of this kind cannot afford to oversimplify the nature and role of existing policies.

The term 'the welfare state' is particularly ambiguous and unsatisfactory and it is unfortunate that the social policies of the post-war years should be popularly summarized by this single expression. The last few decades have seen the development of an intricate and changing complex of welfare provisions, some well known and studied, other less readily observed or identified as social policies. The concept of 'the welfare state', which is popularly used to refer to these changing policies and services, largely reflects the intentions and aspirations of the period of reconstruction, during and immediately after the second world war. As a result of the powerful egalitarian sentiments expressed at the time, the continued use of the expression encourages the view that our society is less unequal than it was during the pre-war years.

Attitudes and beliefs concerning social inequality, its extent, the necessity of and opportunity for reducing it, were of considerable importance in the formulation of policies which cumulatively produced the post-war development of social welfare services. It is perhaps inevitable that the uncritical use of the terms 'welfare state' and 'social services' has encouraged over-optimism concerning the potential of the social welfare system to rapidly create a less unequal society. The generic terms tend to conceal the reality; of services which imperfectly fulfil the intentions and hopes which preceded them. They similarly present a static image of a system of social welfare that has in practice a continually changing impact upon income inequality, due both to variations in the welfare provisions themselves and also in the structure of the society in which they operate.

The continuing trend towards higher average standards of living of the past two decades, combined with the expectations of redistribution mentioned above, has provided a firm basis for complacency about the significance of the fundamental, structural inequalities of society. The resurgence of concern about poverty as a problem of families with children, (in addition to being a problem of old age), has effectively reduced the grounds for such complacency in recent years. Nevertheless, the expectation that social welfare programmes will naturally and effectively reduce inequality requires further study.

It cannot be denied that British social policy has been concerned with redistribution on many occasions and that our social services are, in fact, redistributive.[2] Having said this, however, the important questions remain. It is essential to seek to know what types of social policy and social service are redistributive and why; to know how redistributive they are; in what direction they redistribute; and whether or not the 'welfare state' has become more or less egalitarian in its impact over time.

The expression 'the welfare state' effectively symbolizes the inadequacy, at a conceptual level, of much discussion of social welfare policies and we use it in this book for that very reason. Redistribution studies would have performed a valuable service if they clarified the precise relationship of current social policies to the inequality of income in our society. Such studies might reveal, against one variable at least, the heterogeneity of our social policies and make us more cautious in attributing objectives and achievements to our systems of social welfare provision. But in order to do this such studies must themselves escape the conceptual and definitional problems that we have begun to discuss.

The Concept of Redistribution

One of the most crucial problems to be solved is that of defining 'social policy' and 'social services'. We will discuss this in our next chapter. A concept which has been given less attention by students of social administration is that of redistribution itself. The term is consistently used in this book to refer only to the transfer from one individual (or group) to another, of *income,* or *benefits which may be given some income equivalent.* This is a necessary limitation on its use, though difficulties do arise from placing such limitations upon the concept.[3] The concept is commonly used to imply an income transfer from richer to poorer persons. Indeed, it often carries this implication within this book and it would be tedious to qualify our usage of the term on each occasion. But we need to show whether income transfers do in fact operate in this conventionally assumed direction. Thus the nature and direction of the redistribution process needs on occasions to be closely specified. The most common distinction is that made between horizontal and vertical redistribution, the former referring to income transfers between families with similar gross incomes, but with differing socially recognized needs (i.e. the number of persons dependent upon the income). The latter term may be subdivided for clarity into positive (from richer to poorer) and negative, vertical redistribution. Despite the complexity of the redistribution actually taking place which Nicholson's work has revealed, it would be unwise to pursue definitional distinctions much further at this point.

One further term is needed to make a distinction between social policy objectives and their substantive effects. Some social policies

11

are designed to meet highly specific needs of an otherwise hetero-geneous category of persons. Unless there is a close correlation between the incidence of a specific need and that of poverty or low income, the establishment of provision for that need may not entail vertical redistribution of income. Consequently let us distinguish between 'contingency redistribution' and 'income redistribution'.[4] By the first is meant the transfer of resources between groups of persons which are differentiated only because they are experiencing, or are not experiencing, a particular contingency that attracts social welfare benefits. Thus we can differentiate between the transfer of resources inherent in the provision of social welfare and the transfer of re-sources between identifiable strata within society (income groups or social classes).

All social welfare services entail the transfer of resources and hence contingency redistribution. Redistribution of resources between in-come groups (defined in the sense of vertical or horizontal redistribu-tion) is not necessarily an inherent feature of social services. The basic point to be made is a simple and obvious one. 'No social service programme, whatever its declared or official objectives can be ut-terly neutral in its actual effects on the distribution of income'.[5] The redistribution of resources is an inevitable result of creating a social welfare system, but the redistribution of income from one distinct and easily identified strata of people to another, is not a predictable result. The changes in the distribution of resources may be very complex indeed. We cannot assume that redistribution will necessarily be to the benefit of the poor and we have even less reason to assume that the resulting redistribution has been planned or consciously desired.

Income redistribution may arise in a number of situations none of which constitute inherent features of the provision of social welfare. For example, the socially recognized need may be that of poverty itself or may be very highly correlated with low income. Services organized to meet such needs will tend to result in significant hori-zontal or vertical income redistribution, unless they consist entirely of redistributing individuals' own resources over their life span. Services which are intended to counteract poverty are frequently income redistributive precisely because increased income is the benefit required. Moreover, a society in which a considerable proportion of the population receives low incomes and which provides welfare services for this group, will tend to create methods of financing these services which result in income redistribution. Where poverty is neither so widespread nor severe as to prevent the poor from contri-buting to the cost of social services, these services may still be income redistributive to a significant extent if the concept of equity represented by progressive taxation provides the basis for revenue collection and if the distribution of initial incomes is unequal. Income redistribution will, therefore, tend to occur in the circumstances outlined, even if it is not an integral objective of the social services that are provided. Finally, it is clearly possible that specific decisions may be made to use social services as a means of ameliorating the structural inequalities of a society. In the first three instances income redistribution is seen to be an important or necessary means of attaining contingency redistribution. In the last instance the amount of redistribution sought need not bear any relationship to the amount needed simply to effect a given quantum of contingency redistribution, for the social change being sought relates directly to income inequality.

The relevance of these points becomes clear if one considers the view that redistribution is an inherent feature of the social services.[6] If it is believed that all citizens can purchase most, if not all, of their welfare services, an inherently redistributive system of social services may attract powerful opposition.[7] But it will be clear from what we said above, that contingency redistribution is the only inherent and predictable form of redistribution to arise from the provision of social services per se. British social services may be expected to be income redistributive because of the positive correlation between low income (gross and per capita) and some socially recognized needs; because of the role of progressive taxation as one source of finance for these services; and because of specific commitments to modify the distribution of life chances and styles through social policy. (This last factor is partly expressed in the first two, the choice of needs met by social services and the choice of methods of financing them.) The social services are *not* inherently and permanently agents of substantial redistribution and social change. Some income redistribution may be necessary to obtain any contingency redistribution and contingency redistribution may be organized so as to produce considerable income redistribution, but we are now a long way from making assumptions about the egalitarian effects of our social services.

As we have been implying, there is every good reason to concur with Professor Galbraith's plea for considerable effort to be expended on disentangling the concepts of redistribution and public expenditure.[8] We would agree with him that the former has come to be seen as the inevitable consequence of the latter, largely because of the confused way in which redistribution has been tied to the concepts of 'the social services' and 'the Welfare State'. Nevertheless, we would not suggest, as he has done, that this distinction should be made in order to promote the expansion of public expenditure at the cost of reducing the emphasis placed on redistribution. Conversely, we would urge that redistribution be discussed more frequently and rationally, partly in the belief that it would be easier to assess the need for income redistribution in the future, and partly because present policies need to be carefully evaluated in terms of their redistributive consequences.

We will proceed, therefore, to examine how (if at all) it is possible to arrive at satisfactory measures of the income redistribution effected by social welfare policies and to present a summary in our concluding chapter of the available information on the trends, direction, and extent of such redistribution.

NOTES

1. Barna, T., 'The Redistribution of Income through Public Finance in 1937' Oxford, Clarendon Press, 1945.

Cartter, A. M., 'The Redistribution of Income in Post-War Britain' New Haven, Yale University Press, 1955.

Throughout this book we will refer to 'the work of Nicholson' as a convenient way of noting the published analyses produced by the Central Statistical Office, as much of the pioneering work was conducted by Nicholson. These analyses have been published in 'Economic Trends', November 1962, (1957 and 1959); February 1964, (1961 and 1962); August 1966, (1963 and 1964); February 1968, (1965 and 1966); July 1968, (relating to low income households 1963/66); February 1969 (1967); February 1970 (1968); and J. L. Nicholson, 'Redistribution of Income in the United Kingdom in 1959, 1957 and 1953', reprinted from 'Income and Wealth', Series X.

2. The majority of our final chapter is devoted to giving meaning to this assertion.

3. See Chapter Four.

4. This nomenclature is somewhat confusing because income is transferred in both cases, but the parameters of the transfer are different. In the second case income is being transferred systematically from higher to lower income families (or possibly in the reverse direction). In the first case we are recognizing a movement of resources from a group of persons not suffering a particular contigency to those who are suffering it. In contingency redistribution the *essential and necessary* movement is between these contingency groups and not between income groups.

5. Titmuss, R. M., 'Commitment to Welfare' London, Allen & Unwin, 1968, p. 65.

6. Macleod, I. N. and Powell, J. E., in 'The Social Services: needs and means', (London, The Conservative Political Centre) presented redistribution as a defining characteristic of social services, but they did not define redistribution.

7. The most concerted recent critique of current welfare philosophies presented in the publications of the Institute of Economic Affairs, contains numerous examples; see Seldon, A. and Gray, H., 'Universal or Selective Social Benefits,' London, I.E.R., Research Monograph No. 8.

8. Galbraith, K., in Phelps (ed.) 'Private Wants & Public Needs'; New York, Norton, 1965.

2. FUNDAMENTAL METHODOLOGICAL CONSIDERATIONS

As we have indicated in the first chapter, it is important for the formation of social policy that we obtain adequate measures of income redistribution. It is the aim of the remainder of this book to consider whether any valid evidence has emerged from research studies which can be said to confirm or refute the belief that income inequality is now of less significant proportions than it has been in the past. We have devoted the core of the book to the study of the methodological procedures and problems which affect the validity and relevance of findings on income redistribution.

The redistribution of income is not a neglected area of statistical research in Britain. Compared with any other country we possess a quite substantial amount of information on the operation of redistributive policies. Unfortunately, it is not at all easy to draw firm conclusions from this data, even after allowing for the difficulties of making comparisons between different research projects. The basic research method common to all such studies is easily understood and does not present immediate problems.

The first step in each case is to calculate how incomes (from wages, salaries, rent, interest and other sources such as 'windfalls') are distributed between income receivers and as far as is possible to aggregate these incomes to produce data on the distribution of incomes between families or households. At this point the operation of the tax system (direct and indirect taxes, including national insurance contributions) is excluded and pre-tax income is the concept with which we are dealing. The effect of the social services on incomes is also excluded and transfer incomes (pensions, family allowances and other social security benefits) are not taken into consideration. The resulting data may be usefully referred to as the distribution of *initial* or *pre-redistribution* incomes. The definitions of precisely what constitutes initial incomes and what constitutes a family are complex and open to debate.[1] We will return to these difficulties on a number of occasions in this and the following chapters.

The modification of the initial income distribution by the tax system has to be calculated and the researcher must decide which forms of taxation he considers to be relevant to his study and whether their effects can be assessed with sufficient accuracy. Finally, having allowed for the effects of taxation, the benefits derived from social welfare policies have to be valued in monetary terms and allocated between families or households. The end result is the distribution of income which remains after taxation and social services have redistributed resources. This will be referred to as the distribution of *final* or *post-redistribution* incomes.

The difference between the distribution of initial and final incomes obviously represents the redistribution effected by those taxes and social welfare policies that have been included in the calculations. The findings of redistribution studies are summarized for convenience by income range. Thus, the average initial income of households receiving incomes within a given range of magnitude can be set against their average post-redistribution income. The difference between these two averages represents the amount and direction of redistribution typically experienced by households in that income range. The loss of data involved in averaging the experiences of households is considerably reduced if the data are classified both by household structure (most basically, the number of children in the household) and by income range, this has been done in each of the Nicholson/CSO studies. In the Barna and Cartter studies the data were classified only by income range.

The problem of interpreting the resulting data mainly arises from a few crucial decisions that have to be made by the researcher. These are; the concepts of income and of the family which are to be employed; the assumptions about the incidence of taxation that are to be made; and the way in which welfare benefits are to be translated into monetary terms and allocated to the population.

For the student of social policy the problem of measuring redistribution is one of isolating the impact of a *selection* of all governmental policies on the distribution of incomes. The selection of governmental policies which is chosen represents the concept of social policy employed in the research. In the ideal situation social policy would be rigorously defined and an appropriate grouping of policies would be included in the calculations. There is little evidence that existing researchers have operated this way. A conventional grouping of statutory social services has been included in each of the studies. The social services included do not adequately represent the total range of potentially redistributive social policies, but it must be re-

16

membered that none of the researchers has claimed to study the whole field of social policy.

The other major problem areas in this type of research revolve around the collection of data with which to give substance to the definitions (of income etc.) that have been chosen. In the course of this process ideal definitions and procedures suffer varying degrees of modification. We discuss a number of these problems in this and the following chapter.

It will be apparent that there are many technical hazards to be overcome in measuring redistribution. Moreover, the whole methodology assumes that a series of statistical procedures can in fact isolate the redistributive processes operating within a society. This basic assumption has received little attention but is certainly open to question.[2] Even leaving aside changes in wage levels and differentials, in regional employment opportunities and in social policies which influence the determinants of initial income inequality; there are, therefore, many ways in which different studies may produce differing conclusions about the redistribution effected within our society.

In view of the importance of the distribution of initial incomes, it is worth giving a brief consideration to research which has concentrated solely upon the first stage in the estimation of redistribution. A substantial body of research has centred upon shifts in the equality of the initial income distribution. Dudley Seers stated, in 1951, that 'all distributions show pre-tax income much more equally distributed in 1947 than in 1938, markedly so in the case of distributed personal income' (i.e. excluding undistributed profits).[3] However, his conclusion that there was 'no continuation after 1944 of the previous trend towards the equality of distribution', the coefficient having 'apparently settled down at a level appreciably above (the) pre-war' level, contrasts sharply with the judgment formed by Lydall concerning the following decade. The results of Lydall's research (1959) and also that of Professor Paish (1957) served to indicate the apparent continuation into the later period of the trend towards pre-tax income equality, which Seers had noted in 1951.[4] Indeed, Lydall argued that in the economic situation of the nineteen-fifties there was a permanent bias towards greater equality.

The Board of Inland Revenue had made similar observations on this diagnosed trend with regard to the years 1938 to 1949.[5] De Jouvenel tackled the same problem from a different standpoint and attempted to show that the distribution of income was too egalitarian to permit further substantial levelling between income groups.[6] His demonstration of the non-feasibility of greater equality, consolidates the picture of a remarkably uniform opinion among research workers concerning the growth of initial income equality during the

17

forties and fifties. To complete the statistical picture which had emerged during this period, let us note the findings of the first post-war study of the redistributive effects of social welfare and taxation policy.

As a result of his investigation, Cartter concluded that 'The Dividing Line between persons whose net of taxes and benefits were losers and gainers through this redistribution process was slightly over £400 in 1937 and about £650 in 1948/49. In both years, therefore, about 85-90% of the population are estimated to have gained, although in the post-war years those who gained, gained more, and those who lost, lost more.'[7] Cartter thereby indicated the role of redistribution in enhancing the growth towards equality which the other researches had identified. De Jouvenel alone modified this impression by emphasizing the oblique rather than vertical nature of the redistribution effected by the social services.[8]

However, none of these enquiries were based on data gathered for the specific purpose of research into income inequality and it is this fact which provided the central focal point for the major dissenting criticism of the validity of such research, voiced by Richard Titmuss. In his 'Income Distribution and Social Change' he asserted that the crucial concepts of income, income unit, and also of time, utilized by the researchers had not been examined in detail. His analysis of the methodological inadequacies of initial income distribution studies concentrated on research which depended upon official administrative data, particularly the data arising from the operations of the Board of Inland Revenue.

The methodological critique applied by Professor Titmuss is extended within this book to the three studies of inequality in post-redistribution income which between them represent virtually the entire body of analysis of the impact of the welfare state on income inequality. The first two of these, conducted by Barna and Cartter, depend upon the same administrative data on initial incomes used in the analyses of inequality which Professor Titmuss considered. The latter's cautionary criticism is equally relevant to the initial income bases of these two redistribution studies. The more recent research conducted by J. L. Nicholson, under the aegis of the Central Statistical Office, has utilized data gathered by the Ministry of Labour's surveys.[9] Although the survey data were not collected for the sole purpose of examining income inequality, the studies have introduced a much needed alternative form of investigating both pre and post-redistribution income inequality.

The validity of income inequality studies in relation to Social Policy.

The validity of the research can be discussed in two ways, that is to say a distinction may be made between the 'internal' and 'external' validity of research. In this book the first term will be applied to the validity with which research measures accurately what it purports to be representing, the second term referring to the validity of a study to 'what we are speaking about', to use Wilkins' expression.[10] Cartter, for example, studied the redistributive effects of public expenditure and taxation. The 'internal' validity of his research must be considered in terms of the public finance orientation of his work. But the validity of his findings for the 'external' problem of income inequality in its relation to social policy, is our major concern. As Wilkins notes, it may be the person using statistics that is 'unreliable' rather than the research findings; but within our topic researchers can be held partly responsible for the lack of 'external' validity of their findings with respect to the situations in which they are used.

Before Professor Titmuss' analysis, the validity of initial income distribution data for discussions of social policy had not been formally examined. It is interesting to note that he did not explicitly distinguish between the two aspects of validity. In fact he criticised the distribution studies as if they were specifically designed to meet the needs of social policy. This situation arose precisely because the authors had not delineated the bounds of their work with sufficient diligence and had in part presented their data as if they were immediately applicable to debates on significant social problems.

J. L. Nicholson's work is not furnished with conclusions presented in a form which facilitiates rapid generalization of the results to specific problems. Nevertheless he, along with Barna and Cartter, fails to include a discussion of the suitability of his research for the elucidation of social policy making problems. While acknowledging that income distribution studies have not been conducted, as yet, for the sole purpose of informing and reappraising social policies, we must develop some basic notion of the form such studies could most usefully take.

The conceptual basis of redistribution studies must be appropriate to the area of study in which the findings will be used. If this area of study is social policy the range of social welfare benefits included in the research will be a key determinant of validity. Existing studies have included only publicly financed social services as social welfare benefits and have presented public revenue as the other side of the equation. We have made this general point already. We must now indicate how a public finance orientation can result in an arbitrary selection of benefits and how a broader concept of social policy could be represented in redistribution studies.

Cartter, for example, suggests (as previously quoted) that in both 1937 and 1948, 85-90% (and only this proportion) of the population benefited from the redistributive process. In terms of the algebraic sum of taxes and benefits from the social services, as traditionally defined, this may be an accurate statement. The danger lies in the tendency to generalize from this, that only a similar proportion of the population benefit from social policies. It may be assumed that only this proportion of the population have needs which are socially recognized. Put another way it may be assumed, erroneously, that for at least 10-15% of the population, the recognition of their needs in social welfare policies is financially unimportant to them. Goldman considers that 'more and more people of working age are becoming capable of standing on their own feet', implying that some (the upper income groups) already meet contingencies without the assistance of collective welfare schemes.[11] George Schwartz has epitomized the misrepresentation of social policy aims and practice most cogently in questioning whether it will be necessary 'to subsidize housing for practically the whole population, on the grounds that if they have to pay only twelve shillings a week' for housing it will be 'certain they will all live in a decent home'.[12] In making this statement he fails to indicate that 'practically all the population' are already subsidized. The majority (owner occupiers) receive an invisible, regressive subsidy which he does not consider to be a subsidy precisely because it is concealed. The methodology employed in measuring redistribution may equally conceal the existence of 'subsidies' operating within the tax structure.

If a measure of income redistribution is to be meaningfully related to the redistributive consequences of social policy, the problem arises of defining 'social policy'. Much effort has been expended on seeking satisfactory definitions of this concept and rehearsal of these attempts is unnecessary.[13] What is important is that we should underline the difference in the meaning of 'social policy' and the term 'welfare state' in conventional usage. The latter is used largely to refer to state and voluntary social services, whereas the former, for our purposes, relates to the whole range of social welfare measures regardless of their scope, auspices, or administrative context. The difference is made explicit by distinguishing between *occupational, fiscal* and *social* welfare.[14]

The expression 'social policy' will hereafter be used to indicate welfare activities falling within any of these three categories. Our main concern is with those that governments subsidize in some manner, since state aided redistribtuion is likely in these cases. The term 'social services' refers to the statutory services which comprise the major part of Professor Titmuss' third category of *social* welfare. 'The Welfare State' is a term which may be assumed to refer generally to provision, statutory and voluntary, of the kind summarized by the third category; the term does not seem to be used to refer to fiscal and occupational welfare.

An appropriately designed measurement of redistribution would need to recognize the operation of the fiscal and occupational systems as well as the state social welfare system. Cartter, however, in confining attention to a selection of state welfare services reinforces this conceptual dislocation and provides for the continuation of such misconceptions as those noted in the first chapter.

By measuring redistribution only in terms of what takes place vertically between income groups, Cartter equally fails to quantify the complexity of aim and operation of these state welfare services. An ideal measure of redistribution would reflect the distribution of resources among contingency, as well as income, groups and within the latter, that taking place horizontally as well as vertically.

By including the social costs in terms of hardship and suffering which the benefits are intended to offset or mitigate, it would also be possible to avoid the statistical presentation of a more egalitarian society which results from the increase in a contingency which attracts a social benefit. For example, an increase in the number of homeless families followed by an expansion of provision for them would produce (if financed from general taxation) a statistical movement towards greater equality. Only by concurrently quantifying both needs and benefits would it be possible, more or less automatically, to avoid drawing erroneous conclusions about the nature and necessity of the redistribution process. Valuable as this would be in presenting a more realistic picture of inequality and redistribution in our society, the quantification of some forms of disservices or disabilities (to use Pigou's term) is not yet a feasible undertaking. It is for this reason that we concentrate on adjustments that can be made in the measurement of those aspects of inequality which can be expressed in monetary terms. This study is, therefore, of limited scope in that it excludes from further consideration those phenomena which cannot be quantified. Indeed, it is important to recognize that all income inequality measures remain open to the criticism that they include only a restricted selection of the relevant variables.

An elementary point which is nevertheless of crucial importance may be mentioned at this stage. This is the problem of locating the direction of changes in incomes, in addition to the magnitude of the movement in indices of inequality. Seers provides a useful example of how easily the importance of changes in the distribution may be exaggerated. He states that the 'share (of distributed income) received by the top 10% (of income units) has fallen sharply.[15] On examining his data it is immediately clear that the relative loss by the top 10% of income earners (or rather income units) is far from the unambiguous egalitarian trend he suggested. The decline in the share of the top 1% of incomes is by far the most significant. Such a narrowly located change is subject to far more scepticism on statistical grounds than if it had been more evenly located in the upper income groups. In considering the relevance of such changes for social policy purposes, the distribution of the relative gains among the population of income units is of greater importance. The income units between the 10th and 50th percentile gained an extra 3% of the total income distributed in 1947 compared with their share in 1938, according to Seer's figures. While the bottom 50% of incomes gained between them a mere 1% extra, over the same period. After taxation the respective figures become 5% and 3%. The egalitarian trend which Seers discerned is therefore seen to be a rather trivial gain on the part of the whole of the bottom 50% of incomes and a slightly larger gain on the part of the next 40% of incomes.

Equally, in the study of the redistributive effects of both taxation and social services it is essential that the research design enables us to establish the detailed pattern of change, rather than its mere magnitude and direction. In this respect, Nicholson's classification of income units by family size is a considerable methodological advance which has contributed to the sophistication of his research and will therefore be discussed further. It is worth noting that it is this improvement upon previous studies which permits the statistical emergence of contradictory shifts in inequality. There is some evidence, for example, that an absence of change in the aggregate can conceal changes in the relative advantages conferred by the redistribution process on families of different sizes and composition. These trends may be of greater value to the student of social policy than changes in inequality within the population taken as a whole; but hitherto they have remained undetected due to a lack of sensitivity in the research design. At present such micro-shifts in inequality must be treated with reserve due to methodological problems and the possibility of statistical artefact.

A number of basic points have been made about the design of redistribution studies and these may be conveniently summarized at this point; further consideration is given to each of them in the course of the book. In the first place the basic data on incomes, taxation and the receipt of benefits should be collected for the specific research task in question. Unless this is done the definitions and concepts used in collecting the data may not be appropriate to the task in hand. Secondly, these definitions (of income, etc.) should be appropriate to the situations in which the findings will be employed—in our case the analysis of social policies as agents of redistribution. Thirdly, the full complexity of the redistribution processes should be reflected in the findings, but the findings must obviously be comprehensible. Finally, the process of statistical computation which we are calling a study of redistribution should be conceptually defensible and should not distort or misrepresent the social reality we are seeking to understand. We have in these few obvious criteria a rudimentary yardstick against which to assess the studies that interest us.

One of the difficulties of making methodological criticisms of existing studies of redistribution is that these studies fulfil a number of needs and a single research method cannot be expected to cope adequately with all the demands raised by different types of question. The most useful way to outline the methodological requirements that social policy based questions entail is to list the different types of income redistribution study which would contribute to our knowledge. The six types of study identified below by no means exhaust the possibilities, but they each contain distinctive research problems which we will discuss in the course of the book. Existing studies of redistribution cannot yield the data which would be produced by all of these research designs. Our book is in this sense not only a critique of existing research, but also a statement of the kinds of income redistribution research needed to further the study of social administration.

Alternative methods of measuring Income Redistribution.
1. The net redistributive effect, during a single year, of *some or all taxes and publicly financed social services* could be measured. Published data from numerous sources could be used, or data could be collected through a sample survey (as in the case of Nicholson's research).
2. Estimates could be produced of *all the benefits,* enjoyed by individuals or groups, which may be considered to fall within the sphere of social policy. By concentrating on benefits, customary definitions of the social services need not limit the selection of what are felt to be social policies. Comparisons can be made between the value of different types of benefit attracted by a particular need (for example housing), regardless of the source of the benefit. Such estimates would be of value in presenting a picture of the redistributive potential of the pattern of social recognition accorded to needs.
3. The net redistributive effect (during a single year) of taxation and *all the benefits indicated in 2* could be measured. Such a measure would diverge from that referred to in 1 by including the effects of occupational welfare benefits. The treatment of fiscal (taxation based) benefits raises problems. In existing research they are in-

cluded in the process of estimating the incidence of taxation. An alternative procedure is discussed in chapter five.

4. The level of redistribution could be measured in the way suggested in 1 or 3 for a *series of years*. Changes in the redistributive effect of policies could be identified in this way. This assumes the possibility of on-going research or a series of separate, but methodologically similar studies.

5. Redistribution as specified in 1 or 3 could be estimated through the study of the *life-time* incomes, tax payments and benefit receipts, of cohorts of families drawn from different social groups. This method of study is a very attractive one in that it solves a number of problems which are extremely difficult to overcome in even the most sophisticated studies of the income redistributed during a single year. Much of the income redistributed through the social welfare services is redistributed over time within a family or social groups, rather than between social groups. This affects the findings of existing studies in a number of ways. The benefits (especially pensions) currently being received by particular income groups have been 'earned' by past as well as by current tax payments. This is most obviously so in the case of benefits provided by a 'funded' insurance system, but it is also relevant in the sense that capital investment in the social services proceeds unevenly and current benefits (in all services) reflect past investment as well as current expenditure, to some extent. In addition, the ratio of dependent to non-dependent population varies over time and the distribution of the costs of providing services changes correspondingly. People with similar life chances, but born in different periods, will have experienced varying life time net tax burdens for these reasons.

Moreover incomes change over time and this complicates a study of a single year. Two examples may be given. The income life cycle is such that persons in, say, middle income groups in any one year may be potentially high income earners at the early stages of a career, or high income earners entering retirement (or semi-retirement) on substantial occupational and private pensions. Middle income earners may also be what they appear to be— persons whose incomes will increase relatively little in the future and whose previous incomes were at a comparable or slightly lower level (during their earlier career). Finally, some young earners may enter middle income brackets and suffer a drop to lower income levels for a large part of their working life as skills related to their youth decline. The apparently homogeneous income strata are, therefore, composed of widely divergent sub-groups as far as lifetime earnings are concerned.

24

As will be noted later, Nicholson's study has raised the problem of determining what a person's 'normal' income is during a year (as opposed to the income being received during any one week or month). Considered over a lifetime, there may be no possibility of determining a person's 'normal' income and allocating him to an appropriate income stratum. The net taxation paid by a family means different things depending upon the shape of their graph of lifetime income and the point on the graph occupied at the point of observation and measurement. An extension of this problem illustrates the complication in its most intractable form. As in the example above, a middle income recipient may be a retired person who received a higher pre-retirement income. A middle income earner will be likely to fall within the low income category after retiring from his occupation. Retirement pension benefits allocated to such people will, therefore, appear as benefits accruing to income groups lower than those to which they belonged during their working lives.[16] Low income earners literally receive negligible incomes in retirement before the addition of pensions and cannot be allocated to a meaningful income group. For these reasons the precise effects of income redistribution can only be studied in relation to lifetime experiences. However, the complexity of the research method removes its adoption from the realms of possibility, at least in the foreseeable future. The method is worth discussing mainly as a reminder of the importance of redistribution through time and the distortions that are inevitably introduced by studying the processes of redistribution during a single year.

6. Net income redistribution could also be studied in such a way as to allow for the *cumulative effects of benefits* received, where these can be assumed to exist. The need for this kind of measure is discussed in chapter four. The fact that some benefits increase the recipients' incomes over the passage of time and not merely at the moment of receipt can be readily observed, but it is a difficult phenomenon to reflect in income redistribution studies. As with the previous case the main reason for mentioning the possibility of this form of measurement is to draw attention to the importance of benefits which act cumulatively.

A study of income redistribution and social policy may be concerned with a number of different questions. In the first place, the role of the social services in redistributing resources in the course of a single year, may be the focus of attention. The kind of study involved would fall within category one above; the research undertaken by both Barna and Cartter is of this kind. Their interest was concentrated on the resdistributive effects of public expenditure and taxation and for this reason the social policies which concerned them were the statutory social services. Virtually without exception they excluded occupational welfare benefits and services provided by the voluntary sector, though both these types of provision attract public financial support in some instances. They also failed to emphasize that the taxation system can itself operate to provide welfare benefits to taxpayers. Their research had a public finance, rather than a social policy, orientation.

Until the early nineteen-fifties the evidence on income redistribution was confined to these studies. The very substantial advance made by Nicholson was to design a series of studies based on a single year which cumulatively provide evidence on changes in the rate of redistribution over a period of years. This research therefore falls within our category four. The selection of social welfare benefits included in the research is closely similar to that taken by both Barna and Cartter, but the primary data (on incomes, etc.) are drawn from an entirely different source, as we have already mentioned.

The existing studies clearly address themselves to basically similar questions, but the student of social policy may reasonably feel dissatisfied with the scope of these questions. Our categories of appropriate research methods reflect this dissatisfaction, for they extend or modify the questions that have been asked in existing research. Research falling within our categories two and three (studies of the distribution of social, fiscal *and* occupational benefits) would pose a question which is complimentary to that studied so far, namely, what is the pattern of distribution of *all* collectively provided welfare benefits? This question has received increasing attention in recent years. Comparisons have been made between subsidies provided through the tax system and through social service benefits in such fields as housing, social security and education. However, we have no comprehensive study of the total pattern of recognition accorded to social needs through the fiscal, occupational, voluntary and statutory social welfare systems. Data on the distribution of benefits through all these systems are needed, in conjunction with the findings of existing redistribution studies, if the true complexity of the redistribution process, and of the social recognition accorded to needs, is to be understood.

If attention is focused on the development of the 'Welfare State', that is to say on the development of the major social services since the beginning of the second world war, misleading conclusions would result. It is possible to read into these developments a changing, but fairly explicit concern with social inequality and its reduction through the redistribution of opportunities, resources and therefore income. It may even be possible to present these developments as an attempt to modify substantially the social structure of our society. But as we have noted, the intentions present in the formative stages of all social service policies are diverse and social welfare benefits are not only provided through the statutory social services. No single coherent philosophy is expressed in the totality of social welfare provision. For these reasons the redistributive effects of all welfare benefits must be studied and not merely those provided by the statutory social services.

The two remaining types of research which we outlined above reflect this concern with the complexity of income redistribution. Studies falling within the fifth and sixth categories would examine the operation of social policies over time and the income generating effects of some social services, respectively.

If all these facets of income redistribution had been studied in the past it would be possible to make very detailed and useful analyses of social policy as a source of redistribution and therefore as an agent of social change. By comparison with this ideal situation existing research is very limited in its scope. The Nicholson/C.S.O. studies have made a valuable contribution to our knowledge, but they were not intended to answer all the questions that we have outlined. Our statement of the kinds of research that could usefully be undertaken represents our own interests in this field.

The research undertaken by Barna and Cartter was, as we have indicated, more limited in range and usefulness than the series of findings published by the C.S.O. The problems faced by these two researchers are not merely of historical interest, however, for they place the Nicholson/C.S.O. research in perspective. We have therefore included a brief description of their methods and the difficulties they had to surmount in Appendix I.

The central deficiencies in these early studies are clear enough. Income data were unreliable in themselves, but more importantly did not relate to actual household units. The estimation of taxation based on these income data, was unsatisfactory and in Cartter's case a major form of non-progressive taxation (local rates) was excluded altogether. The allocation of benefits was an even more uncertain process as no comprehensive body of information was available on the distribution of these benefits among the population. At best the assumptions utilized by the researchers tended to reflect the intended consequences of the services rather than their actual impact upon different income groups. In both cases the estimates related only to the distribution and redistribution of income between income groups and not between families of different sizes and composition.

It is singularly easy to be critical of both these studies on methodological grounds and to discount their findings for this reason. The purpose of our comments is to emphasize that basic data on the distribution of incomes, dependents and benefits between income units, must be available if the findings of a redistribution study are to be used with confidence. Both these early studies provided much needed evidence on this subject and most of the methodological weaknesses were unavoidable in view of the deficiencies of these basic data.

By way of contrast, the Nicholson/C.S.O. research was initiated to exploit a new and valuable source of primary data which became available through the operation of the Family Expenditure Survey. These Surveys carried out annually by the Ministry of Labour (now the Department of Employment and Productivity) provide detailed information on the income and expenditure of the families surveyed. The composition of each family is recorded and the use made of some social services by the family is indicated by, or can be inferred from, data collected by the Surveys. The Nicholson/C.S.O. studies compare the amounts which different households pay in taxes and receive in various social service benefits on the basis of the primary data gathered in the Surveys. The difference between the gross taxes borne and benefits received by each household represents net taxation and this positive or negative figure is recorded for different household sizes and incomes in the Nicholson/C.S.O. research.

A number of advantages and disadvantages flow from using survey data as opposed to the 'administrative data' of the Board of Inland Revenue which are discussed in the next chapter.

NOTES

1. A concise and useful discussion of the concept of income is to be found in Cartter, A. M., op. cit., pp. 30–2 and Appendix I includes a short discussion of the methodological problems confronted by both Barna and Cartter. Nicholson, J. L., op. cit., includes a short definition of these concepts of income on pp. 4–5. The most useful critique of these definitional issues is to be found in Titmuss, R. M. 'Income Distribution and Social Change', London, Allen and Unwin, 1962.
2. It has received the critical attention of Alan Peacock and Robin Shannon in 'The Welfare State and the Redistribution of Income', Westminster Bank Review, August 1968. We discuss this problem in Chapter Four.
3. Seers, D., 'The Levelling of Incomes since 1938', Oxford, Blackwell, 1951.
4. Lydall, H., Journal of the Royal Statistical Society, 1959, Vol. 122, Part I; and Paish, F. W., Lloyd's Bank Review, 1957, 43.
5. Board of Inland Revenue, 92nd Report, 1948–9. Cmd. 8052, 1950.
6. De Jouvenel, B. 'The Ethics of Redistribution', Cambridge University Press, 1951.
7. Cartter, A. M., op. cit., p. 79.
8. De Jouvenel, B., op. cit.
9. The 1953 research was based on the Ministry of Labour's Household Expenditure Enquiry of that year and their Family Expenditure Surveys have been used for each of the subsequent years.
10. Wilkins, L. T., 'The Measurement of Crime', British Journal of Criminology, III, No. 4, April 1963, p. 321.
11. Conservative Political Centre 'The Future of the Welfare State', 1957, p. 9.
12. Ibid., p. 25.
13. See for example, Lafitte, F., Inaugural Lecture, Birmingham University; Slack, K. M., 'Social Administration and the Citizen', London, Joseph, 1966; Boulding, K., 'The Boundaries of Social Policy', Social Work, Vol. 12, No. 1. January 1967; and Titmuss, R. M., 'Problems of Social Policy', London, H.M.S.O., 1950; 'Essays on the Welfare State', London, Allen and Unwin, 1963; 'Commitment to Welfare', op. cit.
14. Titmuss, R. M., (1963) op. cit., Chapter 2.
15. Seers D. op. cit., p. 39. The need to locate the direction of change is particularly important when gini coefficients of inequality are used. This problem is emphasized in our final chapter.
16. Nicholson's classification of results by income and family size reduces this problem. Very many retired persons are in one or two person households and they can be distinguished from families with children.

3. THE FAMILY EXPENDITURE SURVEYS AS A BASIS FOR MEASURING INCOME REDISTRIBUTION

As we have already noted the Family Expenditure Surveys are conducted annually and the Nicholson/C.S.O. work has also become a continuous research exercise. Previously, irregular and separately undertaken investigations were the only source of information. It is now theoretically possible to study current changes in income inequality arising from alterations in the incidence of taxation, the provision of benefits, and economic factors which make for movement in the distribution of initial income.

We add the proviso 'theoretically', for the data published in Economic Trends are far less well provided with explanatory notes on methodological details than is Nicholson's book. The latter only relates to the studies conducted in the 1950s. Nevertheless, this is more a reflection upon the quality of the information in the latter than upon the inadequacy of that in the former. The contrast between this service, essential as it is to the effective utilization of the data, and that provided by the Board of Inland Revenue on their surveys of incomes, is marked. Titmuss noted in 1962 that 'less than five pages (had) been devoted (by the BIR) in over twenty years to describing the methods employed in funding for public use the basic data from which all our knowledge derives concerning the distribution of incomes by size.'[1]

A second major advantage of using primary data gathered by survey techniques is that the administrative definitions of income and other basic variables, which restricted the earlier studies, do not have to be relied upon. Moreover, the incidence of taxes and benefits can be based upon the actual circumstances of households and the concept of a household (or family) need not be that employed by the tax authorities.

The concept of income used in the Nicholson/C.S.O. Studies.
Unfortunately, the Family Expenditure Survey does not adopt a

radically different definition of income from that used by the Inland Revenue; in particular capital gains and non-monetary items of remuneration are not included.[2] Their definition certainly fails to approach the concept of income as the 'net accretion of economic power between two points of time.'[3] In 1965 Revell provided evidence of the first quantified movement towards a greater inequality in the distribution of wealth.[4] In view of this, the failure to bridge the income-wealth hiatus is most unfortunate. As Professor Titmuss carefully illustrates, this hiatus is of a conceptual and administrative nature only and it does not extend to current accounting practice.

Nevertheless, it is clear that any attempt to overcome this difficulty (in the context of Nicholson's work) would be of very limited value owing to the sample-based investigation which underlies the study. The extent of mis-reporting of income remains an unknown factor in the existing studies. Any effort to gain information on the value of capital gains (realized and unrealized) would greatly increase the probability of inadvertent error and of non-response among the groups most affected. Indeed, it may be supposed that the concept of income for the individual respondent will be influenced considerably by that which is reflected in his income tax return. The concept of income reflected in the Family Expenditure returns would be unlikely to differ greatly from that in the income tax return whatever the formal definition adopted by the Survey in framing their questionnaire.

The absence of information on wealth and capital gains is an important defect in the Family Expenditure Survey data, but other sources of inaccuracy in income data are apparent. Assessing the incomes of the self-employed is inevitably hazardous. The surveys depend upon statements made by the self-employed regarding the most recent year for which an income figure can be given. It is difficult for the Inland Revenue to obtain accurate returns from this group of income earners, not least because there are often important sources of non-monetary income and business expenses which do not contribute only to business activities. In a voluntary survey the opportunity for incomplete recording of income is very great—this must be assumed to produce some distortion in the survey income data. The survey requests information on goods obtained from householders' own shops and farms, for example, but the likelihood of receiving anything like accurate accounts of such non-monetary income is remote, especially since items of expenditure such as tobacco, alcoholic drink, confectionery and ice cream are noticeably under recorded by the public generally.[5] Moreover, these recorded items of non-monetary income are entered as expenditure but not as income, since income in kind is excluded by the survey. The under-recording of income by the self-employed may be expected to extend to supplementary income earned by persons classed as employees. The understatement of income by women in part-time employment has been noted in the most recent survey report and it may be assumed that other part-time earnings are a likely area of mis-reporting.[6]

The problems of depending upon the voluntary provision by households of income and expenditure information can be illustrated by the lack of reconciliation of income and expenditure data. In 1968 the average weekly expenditure (for all households) exceeded the average weekly income. This is not merely the result of dissaving among pensioners, or temporary dissaving by the high income groups during the particular weeks they were interviewed. Households in all income groups below those receiving a weekly income of £60 or more, recorded higher expenditures than incomes. In most income groups expenditure exceeded recorded incomes by approximately fifty shillings a week and in the highest income group (£60 or more per week) expenditures and incomes were only just in balance. These figures are difficult to interpret with confidence, but given the known tendency to under-record substantially some items of expenditure, it may reasonably be asked whether income recording is accurate. The method of recording data must be expected to produce some discordance between income and expenditure patterns, but the need for caution in using the income data is apparent.

The Family Expenditure Surveys collect information from each of the families which cooperate, for a period of a fortnight (though some items of recorded expenditure relate to longer periods than this). All data on income are then converted into weekly incomes. This period of accounting is the basic unit of time used in the surveys. The Nicholson/C.S.O. studies use a year as their period of accounting and this raises the problem of determining a family's 'normal' income. The short period of time covered by the Family Expenditure Survey may result in the recorded income of a family diverging from what is their 'normal' weekly income. In the case of the self-employed the income for the previous year is determined and this removes the problem of choosing an unrepresentative week, though income received in one year may not be representative of that 'normally' received in the preceeding five or ten years. There are also other difficulties encountered with the self-employed and these were mentioned above.

In the case of salaried workers normal income is not likely to diverge greatly from estimated weekly income except where there are part-time supplementary earnings. The wage earner receiving fluctuating levels of 'take home' pay and persons unemployed or absent from work due to sickness during the weeks of the survey present the greatest problems with respect to assessing normal income. The current practice in the surveys is to request information from employees on the amount of the last payment received and on the amount usually received. The latter figure is used where the two diverge. Where employees have been absent from work but for thirteen weeks or less, their normal income is recorded as above; where they have been away for longer their actual receipts (including social security transfer payments) during the period of interview is recorded. Information on their normal income is therefore excluded from the survey results.

The recording of normal income is obviously crucial to a study of income redistribution and the concept needs closer examination. Wherever possible the tax paid net of benefits by a family should be compared with the families normal position in the income distribution. The Family Expenditure Survey data are inadequate insofar as they cannot easily overcome the problem of widely fluctuating incomes.[7] The very methodology of redistribution studies is undermined by such incomes, for the necessity of classifying households by some concept of normal income may force an arbitrary concept of income receipt upon some families.

Redistribution studies of the Nicholson/C.S.O. kind are possible precisely because most households receive a reasonably steady income. In families where this is not the case, need as well as income may fluctuate considerably. No concept of normal income will fully represent the fluctuations in wellbeing experienced by some families. Though small in number such families warrant much closer study than they have yet received, especially in the context of research into poverty, since low unstable incomes may cause acute problems and they are least easily dealt with through the income transfer services. Such families have to be accepted as a virtually insoluble problem for the nation-wide study of redistribution; and for this reason they would merit examination through a survey specifically designed for this purpose.

Families experiencing long term interruptions of employment also present difficulties and their normal income can be assessed in different ways. On the one hand it can be argued, with the Survey, that after a given period of time (thirteen weeks in the Survey methodology) the normal income of such families is that which they are actually receiving during the period of interrupted work. Grossed up to an annual income this could mean that the estimated annual income reflects the income received during the contingency (implying that the contingency lasts for a full year). Alternatively, it could mean that the estimated annual income is the normal annual income of the family reduced by an amount which represents the actual loss of income incurred during the contingency. The third possibility is to say that even in the case of lengthy contingencies the normal income should be that which the family was receiving *before* the contingency.

At a theoretical level the choice of method can be made on the conceptual appropriateness of each. In the first case one will be measuring the redistribution experienced by a family which is classified by the income received *during the interruption of earnings*. In the second case the measurement is related to an income which also takes account of the interruption of earnings, but over a longer time span (one year) than in the first case. [The first two methods amount to the same thing if the interruption of earnings lasts for a year or more]. The third method only acknowledges the existence of interrupted earnings insofar as this contingency attracts a transfer payment, the net redistribution experienced by the family is compared with the family's pre-contingency position in the income hierarchy.

The choice of solution rests very much upon the purpose of the study and this dilemma underlines the importance of having different types of study each related specifically to the needs, in our case, of social policy analysis. The ideal solution in this instance would be to have all families facing a lengthy interruption of earnings during the survey period analyzed separately, in addition to including them in the main analysis. The benefits received during the contingency could then be related to their initial income (other than transfer payments) during the contingency, their total initial income during the year, and in the case of contingencies lasting for very substantial periods, their normal income in the last full year before the onset of the contingency. Only in this way would it be possible to determine the effectiveness of *contingency redistribution* through taxation and benefits *and* the impact of *income redistribution* on the structural inequalities of the society.

The retired person presents this kind of problem in acute form. Nicholson faced a real dilemma in dealing with pensioners since many households consisting of elderly people have negligible initial income and they automatically fall into the lowest income category. Classification by the pre-retirement normal income of the household, though exceedingly difficult, would be a very satisfactory solution in theory. It would permit comparisons between pre- and post-retirement income inequality. Nicholson's solution was to exclude pensioner households (with no substantial initial income) from the general analysis.

In view of the first problem we tackled (the 'normal' income of the pre-retirement population), it should be noted that some employees may retire before becoming entitled to a state retirement pension and in the interregnum they may receive transfer payments because of the loss of earnings incurred. The pre-contingency income of such households is particularly important since their retirement income will place them low in the income hierarchy at a time when they will not be classified as retirement pensioners, but when they may be receiving cash benefits.[8]

In practice the resolution of the normal income dilemma has been influenced by factors other than the theoretical considerations discussed. The survey samples have never been large enough to warrant the degree of sophistication suggested above and the problem of gathering reliable data on pensioners' pre-retirement normal incomes are so considerable that such an approach would not be realistic in the context of the Family Expenditure Survey. In the early years of Nicholson's work data were not systematically available on the normal incomes of those persons away from work during the period of the survey. Nevertheless, the normal income of some of these people was known. Such information has been used, in preference to actual incomes received during the survey period, wherever available and in the later studies it must be assumed that normal income is the usual basis for classifying such families. The number of families in which data on normal income are inadequate, or in which the concept is inappropriate due to lengthy interruptions of work, is not discussed by Nicholson and the method of dealing with these families is not known.

Finally it must be noted that the concept of normal income as we have been using it is largely tied to a one year period of accounting and is entirely so in the case of the Survey and Nicholson/C.S.O. studies. But we have touched upon the unrepresentativeness of even a yearly average income. Some households, especially some of the self-employed, may experience considerable income fluctuations from year to year, while all employees experience some kind of life-income cycle. To measure the effect of income redistribution (and therefore of social policy) on structural inequality requires the use of life-time incomes, or at the very least knowledge about the position of each income earner and each household in their life-income cycle and the approximate 'shape' of that cycle. Ideally the normal life-income (the average annual income over the whole working life) should be compared with the actual income in the year of each survey; this alone would permit definitive statements to be made on the egalitarian effects of income redistribution.

The normal life-income would also be necessary if one were to eliminate the effect of redistribution through time. That is to say longitudinal studies of benefits received and taxes paid over lifetimes could indicate how far income is distributed *between* different life-income groups and how far it is simply redistributed over time *within* life-income groups. As we acknowledge in our concluding chapter, these types of study are not likely to be developed, but discussing them serves to illustrate the severe limitations of those studies which are presently both feasible and undertaken.

Despite all the problems that we have mentioned there is some evidence that the *basic* data on incomes collected by the Survey are not greatly misleading. Thatcher has indicated that during the years 1963-66 the normal weekly earnings for manual workers recorded by the survey were on average only 1% less than the earnings recorded in the Ministry of Labour earnings enquiries. By grossing-up Survey data he was able to compare a total wage and salary bill with the comparable sum recorded in the national income statistics.[9] The deficiency in Survey data was 4.9% for 1963 and only 0.7% for 1966, on this basis. The reliability of the Survey's income data seemed to be improving during the mid-sixties to judge by these estimates and the discrepancies were certainly acceptable ones in 1966. Despite this fact, some additional discrepancies do arise from part-time and additional earnings (especially among women) and data on higher incomes are less reliable than those on average incomes.

The Concept of the Family or Household.

We have been using the terms 'income unit', 'family' and 'household' interchangeably in the preceeding passages and for Nicholson's study this is far more justifiable than with the previous studies. The 'household' is used as both an income and expenditure unit in the Family Expenditure Surveys in contrast with the income recording units of the Board of Inland Revenue which bear no known relation to expenditure units. The definition of the household used in the Survey is similar to that used by the Population Census.[10] The Survey questionnaires request details of the income of all members of this social grouping. The Survey therefore provides, within the limits of accuracy of reporting, the total income of a unit whose actual composition and expenditure pattern is known. Unfortunately the household as a unit is not necessarily one which pools income and shares expenditure. The family consisting of single people, couples or couples with children[11] is the concept which would probably have been selected, were it not for the practical difficulties. For example, young adult offspring who are sharing the parental home before marriage may participate only partially in the budgeting of the rest of the family. Married children, lodgers and families sharing accommodation may be presumed to be financially independent of the rest

35

of the household. Households consisting of groups other than single people, single people with children, couples and couples with children represented 28.2% of all households in 1964.

Moreover, only private householders are included in the survey thus excluding people living in institutional, boarding house and hotel accommodation. This omission would only be likely to affect the results marginally, towards the upper end of the income scale in so far as hotel residence is concerned, and the lower end of the income scale with respect to quasi-institutional residences. Nevertheless in the lower income ranges full institutional care (in the form of treatment and residence benefits) may constitute a high proportion of the final income of many persons. That the exclusion of these income groups is not unimportant can be seen by the distinctly non-random sample of the population which Townsend, for example, found in his study of residential care for the aged.[12] The population in this case was strikingly non-random with respect to personal variables of age, mobility and previous family structure. This example illustrates the danger of generalizing about the direction of redistribution. While the single person may be expected to contribute through taxation towards the needs of the married couple with children in some situations, there is a clear reversal of this process in the case of institutional care.

The connotations that attach to the concept of redistribution are also seen to need closer examination. Any increase in institutional care would tend to produce a statistical movement towards greater equality, or at least towards a higher level of income redistribution. This would reflect a real increase in equality if the provision for the contingency rather than the incidence of the contingency was increasing. Alternatively, such a statistical move towards greater redistribution may be accompanied by a rising incidence of hardship, as for example when more elderly persons become isolated in extreme age or frailty and require expensive, though not necessarily satisfactory, residential care. This example, therefore, confirms the importance of the distinction we made earlier between contingency and income redistribution. An expansion in the provision of social welfare services increases the sum total of income transferred within the society during a given period of time. This increase in income transferred does not necessarily imply a move towards greater income equality.

In such a situation an holistic measure of *welfare*, such as we referred to earlier, would help reflect the true nature of the change as a mitigation of an existing inequality in well being, rather than as a financial bounty to a reasonably affluent group of a not so markedly more affluent society. The latter is the first interpretation that might be placed upon such a change by some critics. Nicholson's study does not in any sense depart from the quantification of the purely monetary aspects of inequality and redistribution. Nevertheless his analysis by both family composition and income is one step towards a more explicit delineation of the social characteristics of beneficiaries as opposed to their purely financial status. This refinement applies to data relating to a majority, but not all, of the population. In recent years a little under 10% of the sample has consisted of households which have been excluded from the analyses due to their poor representation. In addition the sample does not quite cover the whole population of interest to us.

The Problem of Non-Response.

Apart from the under reporting of incomes, the most obvious disadvantage of using Family Expenditure Survey data is that of bias arising from non-response. Nicholson has confirmed that a comparison with Inland Revenue data reveals that non-response has been most prevalent in the highest and lowest income ranges.[13] The small number of respondents from the highest income group was evident in both 1957 and 1959, and the adjustment for non-response is correspondingly large relative to the number of respondents in this income range.[14] The adjustment for non-response is particularly crucial in studying inequality, since measures of inequality are especially sensitive to changes occurring at the extremes of the distribution. A short description of the methods of adjustment used during the earlier studies is included as Appendix 2. In 1963 the attempt to reweight the sample and reduce the impact of non-response was abandoned—it has not been re-employed. Since the fifties the rate of non-response has fallen somewhat and the current response rate is close to 70%. This is a good response rate for such a complex survey and the reliability of results should have improved in the last few years due to an increase in sample size in 1967.[15] The sampling errors in the new, larger surveys are certainly small enough to be easily tolerated. Mogridge has estimated the errors within the distribution of households and concluded that in 1967, even at the extremities of the distribution, the error is fairly small and it is therefore 'possible to be confident that there is a high probability of accuracy'.[16] The error was larger in the smaller sample of 1966 and presumably the same was true in the years prior to 1966.

The improvements in the sample have been reflected in the greater coverage given to the minority groups of households. Low income households have been analyzed in greater detail in recent years and households of one or two adults are now presented in some tables as falling within three categories; pension households; non-pensioner, retired households; and non-pensioner, non-retired households.[17] The enlarged 1967 sample also contained, for the first time, a reasonable number of households receiving incomes in excess of £3,000 per annum.

These improvements do not remove the fundamental problem of bias. Even in the 1967 sample the number of responding households with original incomes in excess of £3,100 was a mere 359, out of a total sample of 7,386: there were only eleven respondents with incomes in excess of £8,055. The findings for this first year of the enlarged sample are virtually meaningless for income ranges above £3,100. Results are in fact grouped for all incomes above this level and they therefore refer to a very broad band of incomes. Mogridge has produced a very useful estimate of the probable bias* in income data resulting from non-response. He argues that the Family Expenditure Survey mean income was some 5.8% too low due to non-response in 1963. At the highest income levels this rises to 14%.[18] This estimate of bias does not include the effects of under-reporting of income. The data on higher income groups are clearly more suspect than those for the middle ranges of income.

The 1967 results were more acceptable for large families than they were for large income households, in that there was a useful number of respondents with four children in five different income ranges. Larger families than this remain unrepresented in the detailed analyses. In 1964, with a smaller sample, the position with regard to high income groups was very similar to that in 1967, but four children families were virtually unrepresented and even three children households were poorly represented. Moreover, deficiencies in the representation of important sub-groups have been noted by Abel-Smith and Townsend with respect to the earlier surveys. In the years 1953-54 and 1960 they discovered that 'the proportion of children was 12-13% greater than would have been expected from national figures.'[19] The number of aged persons was under-represented in both years and the number of sick heads of households was very substantially under-represented in 1953. Not surprisingly there was a considerable under-representation of households receiving national assistance in this year and Abel-Smith and Townsend rightly stress the under-statement of the number of households with low standards of living that occurred in both years.

In view of the difficulties to be faced in using Family Expenditure Survey data, this method of studying our subject is not immediately more satisfactory than using existing Inland Revenue statistics. The sample of households included in the Surveys is relatively small and the results are subject to the normal errors in probability sampling. Indeed the additional problems, especially of non-response, involved

---

* The word 'bias' is used to mean 'statistical bias' throughout the text.

in any non-obligatory sample are, or may be, a considerable source of bias. Notwithstanding the small payment offered to respondents, non-response has been a considerable problem; that is to say the samples are not random in practice.[20]

Against this must be weighed the advantage of a survey which, if random or nearly so, will reflect social changes in the size and composition of the income-expenditure unit (the household). Inland Revenue statistics fail to illustrate such changes. They also, due to the definition of an income unit that is employed, present changes in the income recording unit as if they were changes in the level of income received by household units of presumably stable structure. That is to say a trend towards submitting separate income returns for husbands and wives or children, in so far as these are not successfully 'married', appears as a change in the distribution of income in the case of Inland Revenue data. This advantage of the sample survey basis of Nicholson's work is but one aspect of the more general methodological advance made possible by the survey, namely the classification of results in terms of both income range and the structure of actual household income units. The main advantages of using Family Expenditure data arise from the allocation of taxation and social service benefits to households.

The allocation of Taxation and Benefits.

Taxation.

The advantage of a survey based study with respect to taxation is that information is obtained on taxes actually paid by socially significant income units, (households). Indirect taxation is allocated by reference to the recorded expenditure of the household during the fortnight of the survey.[21]

The recording of expenditure over a period of only two weeks raises difficulties for expensive items of a non-recurrent nature are purchased by some sample households. The amount of tax payable on private motor vehicles, for example, is sufficient to produce embarrassing statistical anomalies when allocated to a family type of a given income range. The information accompanying the publication of findings in Economic Trends includes a brief reference to this difficulty and the methods used to overcome it in 1961 and subsequent years. Large amounts of indirect taxation on motor vehicles bought outright (or with a large down payment) during the fortnight covered by the survey, are in fact distributed among the same and adjacent income cells of the type of family making the purchase. Thus in some cases the taxation allocated to one cell is reduced to avoid the effects of unusually large items of expenditure, though at the expense of modifying the household expenditure patterns recorded by the survey. While this solution is not completely satisfactory, it will be seen that the data on expenditure nonetheless permit a more sophisticated analysis than was possible in previous studies.

During the early years of the research no attempt was made to assess the cost to consumers of taxation on intermediate products.[22] The result is the presentation of the algebraic sum of taxes and benefits in a more favourable form for each household, than would be warranted by actual expenditures and receipts. The effect on the redistribution between different income-family groups during these years remains an unknown factor, but such taxes have been included in the later studies and are estimated to be mildly regressive in their incidence.[23]

The potential advantages of the expenditure survey as a means of allocating taxes is not to be minimized in view of the considerable problems which the utilization of independent research findings presented to both Barna and Cartter. However, the size of the samples and the necessarily limited period over which expenditure is recorded by each family, makes caution necessary when interpreting such detailed analyses as those which Nicholson has produced.

A far more fundamental reason for caution is advanced by Peacock and Shannon.[24] As they note the Nicholson/C.S.O. methodology tends to treat the allocation of taxes and benefits as a purely statistical problem. The theoretical objections to the adoption of any one set of assumptions in the process of allocation, are profound. While not ignoring the theoretical questions, Nicholson's pioneering work involved the development of statistical methods of quantification based on only one set of assumptions. The studies have not included sets of findings based on alternative ideas about the most appropriate bases for allocating taxes or benefits. 'What justification is there', as Peacock and Shannon note, 'for the C.S.O. procedure of assuming that direct taxes, such as income tax and national insurance contributions, are fully borne by income-receivers and that taxes on expenditure, such as purchase taxes and excises, are fully passed on by producers to consumers of taxed goods?'[25] In our opinion the importance of developing the research was sufficient justification for the initial decision to establish a single set of assumptions. But the C.S.O. studies have reached a stage where alternative criteria and results would be a valuable recognition of the theoretical problems underlying their methodology.

While we agree with Peacock and Shannon on the difficulties arising in allocating taxes, we would not detect, as they do, 'a curious, old fashioned Marxist tinge' about the choice of taxes allocated. They imply that Nicholson treats taxes on wealth and profits, which

40

'are borne by rentiers and capitalists—unproductive members of society—(as if) they are of no consequence in any calculation of society's welfare.'[26] The choice of taxes allocated in the studies partly reflects the availability of data on each form of tax, but the studies are firmly based on income and not capital. It is unfortunate that the taxes referred to are excluded.

The *ownership* of capital is equally unrepresented in the studies. The inclusion of all capital account considerations, wealth, related taxes and the capital assets and investment effects of the social services, would be welcome. The more privileged members of society are not treated differentially by the research methodology with respect to only the one item, taxation. In the long run it would be far more satisfactory if the C.S.O. studies met the criticisms raised by Peacock and Shannon. Taxation could be allocated on several sets of assumptions producing alternative estimates of income redistribution. The most difficult problem would be to reflect the ownership and redistribution of capital. It cannot be denied that ignoring the processes of redistribution of capital assets is statistically convenient, but fundamentally unsatisfactory at a theoretical level.

Benefits.

Nicholson divided these into direct and indirect benefits. Direct benefits are national insurance payments, family allowances, non-contributory pensions, national assistance grants, school meals, milk and welfare foods, state education, the national health service benefits, and grants and scholarships from local and central government. The indirect benefits comprise food subsidies benefiting consumers (in 1957 only) and housing subsidies. Cartter and Barna allocated a comparable group of benefits. With the exception of Cartter's exclusion of locally financed services, no dramatic problems of comparability arise between the studies through the choice of benefits to be allocated. This cannot be said of the methods of allocation which, as we have already seen, raise important questions for social policy. Nicholson's assumptions in some cases indicate the continuing paucity of information on the differential use and quality of service by socio-economic class. They also give rise to some major theoretical considerations and, for this reason we will discuss the allocation of benefits separately in the fifth chapter.

NOTES

1. Titmuss, R. M., 1962, op. cit., pp. 28–9.
2. Nicholson, J. L., op. cit., pp. 14–15. Capital gains, undistributed profits, tax evasion and avoidance were not allowed for in the data utilized. Income in kind is included in principle, but in practice little more than rent free accommodation is included. The exclusion of institutional populations from the sample in itself removes a number of incomes in kind from the calculations. Some data are gathered and published on the receipt of free and concessionary goods, but the sums involved are very small and the reporting of these items is liable to be erratic. Department of Employment and Productivity, Family Expenditure Survey Report for 1968, p. 116, para. 1 3 and Table 3, pp. 16 and 17.

3. Report of the Royal Commission on the Taxation of Profits and Income, 1952–5, Cmnd. 9474. Memorandum of Dissent by Messrs. Kaldor, Woodcock and Bullock, p. 355.

4. Revell, J. R. A., Report to the Annual Meeting of Economic Historians Association, Munich 1965. Unpublished.

5. Family Expenditure Survey Report for 1968, p. 2, para. 12 and p. 117, para. 16.

6. ibid., p. 3. para. 14.

7. Casual workers and individuals joining or retiring from the labour force within a particular year complicate the picture and a useful distinction can be made between 'full-year workers' and 'part-year workers'. For further discussion of these problems see Thatcher, A. R., 'The distribution of earnings of employees in Great Britain', Journal of the Royal Statistical Society, Series A., Vol. 1331, No. 2, 1968.

8. This group will also be small in number but there is good reason to concentrate attention on each of the groups of households where the estimation of normal income is a considerable problem.

9. Thatcher, A. R., op. cit., pp. 144–6.

10. The household was defined as all persons occupying the same dwelling and catered for by the same person(s), including domestic servants and children at boarding school. Ibid., p. 3.

11. Children are defined as being under the age of 16.

12. Townsend, P., 'The Last Refuge', London, Routledge and Kegan Paul, 1963.

13. Nicholson, J. L., op. cit., p. 62.

14. Ibid., Tables XI and XII, pp. 50, 53. The number of respondents in the income range of £2,600 and over was thirteen in 1957 and 33 in 1959. The total numbers of respondents in these years were 2,817 and 3,092 respectively.

15. Economic Trends, February 1969. The samples yielded approximately 3,000 fully responding households until 1967 when the number rose to 7,000. The effective sample in 1968 consisted of 10,400 households, the response rate was 69% and the number of respondents (i.e., households co-operating) was just over 7,000. See the Family Expenditure Survey Report for 1968, p. 1.

16. Mogridge, M. J. H., 'Household Income and Household Composition', Centre for Environmental Studies, Working Paper, No. 29.

17. Economic Trends, February 1969 and February 1970. The distinction between pensioner and other retired households is based on income factors. Pensioner households are those without significant incomes from sources other than state financed transfer payments.

18. Mogridge, M. J. H., op. cit., p. 22.

19. Abel-Smith, B., and Townsend, P., 'The Poor and the Poorest'. Occasiona Papers on Social Administration, No. 17, London, Bell, 1965.

20. Nicholson, J. L., op. cit., pp. 15–16.

21. Local rates, licence duties, telephone, gas and electricity accounts and a few other items have been recorded for longer periods than a fortnight.

22. The treatment accorded to the various forms of taxation in the Nicholson/C.S.O. studies is discussed in the articles published in 'Economic Trends,' op. cit., and in Nicholson, op. cit., pp. 9-14.

23. Economic Trends, February 1969.

24. Peacock, A., and Shannon, R., 'The Welfare State and the Redistribution of Income'. Westminster Bank Review, August 1968.

25. Ibid., pp. 43 and 44.

26. Ibid., p. 38.

4. THE FINDINGS OF THE NICHOLSON/C.S.O. STUDIES: A CRITIQUE

In this chapter we will discuss the results published for 1964 in detail, but modifications incorporated in the C.S.O. studies since 1964 are noted at appropriate points in the text. The estimates made in 1964 are more likely to be accurate than those made in earlier years and they relate to the same period as our own estimates, which we discuss in Chapter 6.[1]

The following assumptions underly Nicholson's work and the value of his findings is dependent upon them.

(1) Employers' National Insurance contribution have been regarded as part of employees' incomes and as a tax on these incomes.[2]

(2) Retail prices are assumed fully to reflect personal and indirect expenditure taxation.

(3) On average, and after allowing for expenditure by the non-household population not covered by the Family Expenditure Survey, about 50% of the taxes on alcohol and 25% of the taxes on tobacco remain unaccounted for. Expenditure on these items has been increased to allow for these discrepancies. Similar but smaller adjustments are also made to reported expenditure on confectionery, soft drinks and ice-cream.

(4) The notional income accruing from owner-occupied premises is assumed to be equal to their rateable value.

(5) Death duties and taxes on company undistributed profits have been disregarded and undistributed profits have not been allocated to income groups. (Barna and Cartter included this item).

(6) War pensions and service grants are included in benefits.

(7) Allocable benefits consist of national insurance payments, family allowances, non-contributory pensions, national assistance payments (now supplementary pensions and benefits), school meals, milk and welfare foods, state education, educa-

tional and housing grants and subsidies from central and local government, and the national health service benefits.

(8) Only items of government expenditure specified in (7) have been deemed to be benefits. Other items, such as expenditure on defence or on parks, have been disregarded.

Taxation and benefits as a proportion of original income for 1964 is shown in Table (1) for different household types. Income ranges above £2,122 account for approximately 13% of households. These were excluded because the number involved are insufficient to provide a reliable sample. As the data are derived from the Family Expenditure Survey, household, rather than family, income is used. Average annual household income in 1964 was £1,224. Accordingly, average incomes were about midway between the £988/£1,196 and £1,196/£1,448 ranges.

The following conclusions are apparent from the table:

(1) A large share of total taxation is represented by indirect tax.

(2) Although the amount of indirect tax borne rose with incomes, the rise was less than proportionate. Accordingly, this taxation was regressive for all household sizes. This is especially so in the case of domestic rates, as was confirmed by the Allen Report.[3]

(3) Because of the inclusion of flat rate National Insurance contributions, direct taxation is only mildly progressive within the ranges listed.[4]

(4) Total taxation is generally slightly regressive. This is, of course, the result of the mild progression of direct taxation being insufficient to outweigh the regression of indirect taxation.

(5) Benefits are progressive, the lower the income the larger the proportionate benefits. A substantial part of the benefits, particularly for adult households are cash benefits (National Insurance and other social security benefits) which constitute a large proportion of the income of small income households. National Health Service benefits are the main source of benefit in kind received by families without children. In the case of households with children, benefits in kind, including education and National Health service, are important. These benefits are also progressive.

(6) Net tax (taxation less benefits) is progressive, but only mildly so, except for the two lowest income ranges. In the case of two adult households, net tax rises to 28% for income range (d), which is approximately average income, and remains constant for the remaining income ranges. For households with children, progression carries on in all income ranges, but not very markedly.

(7) The difference in the burden of taxation for the three house-

TABLE 1—Taxation and Benefits per Household Income and size—1964
% of Income

	(a)	(b)	(c)	(d)	(e)	(f)	(g)
Income Range	559/ 676	676/ 816	816/ 988	988/ 1,196	1,196/ 1,448	1,448/ 1,752	1,752/ 2,122
Median Income	626	750	904	1,100	1,323	1,581	1,931
2 adults							
Direct tax	14.0	15.6	15.4	16.8	15.9	17.1	17.8
Indirect tax	21.0	18.9	18.0	17.4	16.8	15.6	13.5
TOTAL TAX	35.0	34.5	33.4	34.2	32.7	32.7	31.3
BENEFITS	(23.7)	(18.3)	(9.4)	(5.9)	(3.1)	(4.4)	(2.5)
Total tax less benefits	11.3	16.2	24.0	28.3	29.6	28.3	28.8
2 Adults, 1 child							
Direct tax	11.1	12.8	13.7	13.2	13.4	15.5	18.9
Indirect tax	21.4	19.9	18.0	17.5	15.8	16.0	16.8
TOTAL TAX	32.5	32.7	31.7	30.7	29.2	31.5	35.7
BENEFITS	(25.8)	(19.5)	(15.0)	(11.7)	(8.9)	(8.4)	? (5.1)
Total tax less benefits	6.7	13.2	16.7	19.0	20.3	23.1	30.6
2 adults, 2 children							
Direct tax	10.5	10.8	9.7	11.3	12.0	12.6	15.3
Indirect tax	22.7	20.9	19.6	18.3	15.3	15.7	14.2
TOTAL TAX	33.2	31.7	29.3	29.6	27.3	28.3	29.5
BENEFITS	(31.4)	(26.6)	(22.6)	(17.9)	(14.0)	(14.8)	(12.8)
Total tax less benefits	1.8	5.1	6.7	11.7	13.3	13.5	16.7

Source: This Table is a condensed presentation of the C.S.O. findings for 1964. Economic Trends, August 1966.

hold sizes is small. Households with two adults in income range (d) pay 34.2% of their income in tax. For households with two adults and one child the proportion falls to 30.7% and when there are two children to 29.6%. The benefits, especially benefits in kind, for households with children rise substantially. Accordingly, in income range (e) households consisting of two adults and one child pay 67% of the net taxation paid by two adult households. When there are two children the ratio falls to 41%.

At low incomes the ratio of net tax paid by households with children to that paid by two adult households is noticeably more favourable to the households with children than it is at higher incomes. This reflects the fact that two adult households with average and above average incomes bear a proportionate amount of net tax. (i.e. it is not very progressive while net tax is distinctly progressive for households with children). The same phenomenon occurs with one adult households in all income ranges, listed but in these households net tax becomes proportionate at a considerably lower income.

The number of households with three children is very small in the 1964 sample and they are listed only in income ranges (b) and above. Direct taxation is, of course, lower for this type of household because of children's allowances and cash benefits rise as a result of family allowances. Benefits in kind are also greater. Accordingly, in income range (d) benefits exceed tax by 2.0% and in range (f)—the highest listed—net tax is only 3.9% of original income. The proportion of three children households with incomes lower than (b) is 14%.[5] For these low income households direct taxation is proportionately higher, because of the fairly constant element of National Insurance contributions. The incidence of benefits is, however, progressive.

The top 13% of household incomes, those in ranges higher than (g) are only very partially covered by the study. Except for the bottom 39% of incomes of one adult and bottom 31% of two adult households, the net tax burden was almost proportionate over all income ranges and only in the lowest incomes was net taxation progressive. About 60% of all households consisted of adults only.

In the case of one child households, net tax was progressive for the bottom 40% and the top 3% of incomes. For two child households the bottom 35% of incomes bore progressive net taxation. For other one and two child households tax burdens were fairly proportionate.

Comparing households of average incomes but of different household size, two adult households' net tax burden was lower than that of one adult households by 2% of income. Similarly, in households with one or two children, net tax was respectively 9% and 16% of incomes less than it was in two adult households. Thus, a wife or husband was 'worth' 2% and a child 8% of income. In the case of three children households the reduction in net tax burden per child was higher. The reduction for families with lower incomes was smaller.

Criticism of the Results

Nicholson's study purports to show that, except for the top 13% of incomes excluded, taxation is regressive for the lowest income groups and thereafter proportionate. *Net taxation* is progressive for the lowest incomes and thereafter almost proportionate. The same phenomenon occurs for each of the three household sizes reviewed. Net taxation borne by households with children was substantially lower in all income ranges than for adult only households.

Merrett and Monk,[6] using Inland Revenue average data for all family sizes, reached similar conclusions about the regression of taxation borne by the lowest income groups and the proportionality of taxation and net taxation borne by the others. These findings have now been generally accepted and policies advocated as a result.

However, we would contend that, despite his major contribution to the study of this subject, Nicholson's conclusions are still of limited value for the reasons outlined in this chapter and in chapter five.

(a) *The allocation of National Insurance and other Cash Benefits*

These benefits amounted in 1965 to £2,033 million—40% of all benefits and 20% of all government expenditure. Of this sum £245 million is accounted for by supplementary pension benefits, which, by their very nature, are made available only to the lowest income groups. The major part of the remaining expenditure was distributed as retirement pensions. Incomes of the retired are considerably lower than average. There were nine times as many household incomes of under £10 per week when the head was over sixty-five as when he was under that age. Similarly, widows' pensions and unemployment benefits are, on average, received by low income groups.

As a result, cash benefits, which include family allowances and war pensions, are much higher for the lowest income groups and tend to reduce the burden of net taxation. This is especially so for households consisting only of adults, where the proportion of pensioners is highest. Thus, for a two adult household in the initial income range £315 to £382, cash benefits amounted to £294, whereas in the range

£1,448 to £1,752 they were only £10. Even in income range (b) (see Table 1) they were ten times higher than in range (f). Thus, the 'benefits' *attributed* to a two adult household where National Insurance pensions or grants are *not* being received are substantial. If cash benefits are excluded net taxation for two adult households in range (b) rises from 16.2% (Table 1) to 27.3%, whereas in range (f) it rises from 28.3% to only 28.9%. Accordingly net taxation for adult households of employed and not retired heads of households was really proportionate for these income groups and not progressive as the C.S.O. study indicates. This problem of averaging the experience of one type of household to other types is an unavoidable result of the research method.

(b) *Employers' National Insurance Contributions*

Employer's National Insurance contributions have been added to income and also included in direct taxation. It can be argued that these, in fact, constitute an indirect expenditure tax. These are taxes paid by manufacturers and traders which enter into the cost of the product. They are, therefore, passed on to the consumer in the retail price and are indirectly borne by him. National Insurance Contributions, if included in this category, constitute the largest tax of this kind. The National Income Blue Book includes National Insurance contributions in personal income taxes and adds them to personal income. In conditions of perfect competition, it is probably that much of this tax would be borne by employees. However in present conditions of trade union bargaining it would seem more probably that they are mainly borne in the first instance by the employer and eventually passed on to consumers.[7] The Selective Employment Tax is of the same nature.

(c) *Additional Income*

A number of items could logically be included in the figures of original income. Ideally all forms of non-monetary remuneration would be included under this heading in order to provide a more realistic measure of initial income. The limitation in this case, as we have already noted, is essentially the technical one of gaining reliable data on such income from a sample survey.

At least two forms of additional income not included in the C.S.O. studies can be estimated and we include these in our own calculations in Chapter six; they are employers' superannuation contributions and the full value of imputed rent accruing to owner occupiers. The C.S.O. do not include employers' contributions because they include the pensions, where paid, instead. To include both would be to count the value of this item twice. In Chapter six we are able to include employers' contributions without facing this problem, precisely because we have constructed estimates for a few types of family circumstance not separately analysed by the C.S.O. and we do not attempt to make global estimates. This is an example of the contribution that supplementary estimates can make.

Consideration of these forms of income in isolation is not very helpful, however, as they are closely related to benefits and tax concessions accruing to persons with these same welfare needs. We shall proceed therefore to estimate the value of these forms of additional income while considering the principal benefits and tax concessions arising in the areas of housing and pensions and life assurance. These two sections, plus a third section on the tax treatment of self-employed and the operation of capital gains tax are included as case examples of the complexity with which the main variables in any redistribution measure, initial income, wealth, social and occupational welfare benefits, tax concessions and additional income, are related.

(d) *Housing*

Housing is treated in an illogical and half-hearted way in national income and expenditure statistics. One man may pay rent of £2 per week for a satisfactory house and another £3 for an insanitary tenement. Because this factor cannot be taken into account, no true comparison can be made of the distribution of economic resources between the two. The market in housing, at least since 1919, has been an imperfect and distorted one. Control of private rents and subsidized local authority and owner-occupied housing have brought about radical changes in the real, but not recorded, incomes of different groups of people.

Nevertheless, it is possible to explore the redistribution of income produced by housing policies. The three main types of housing at December 1964 are shown in Table (2).

(i) *Local Authority Housing*

The amount of Exchequer subsidy per new house has varied over the years. Subsidies for sixty years were fixed at a specified amount for each new house built. Larger sums were payable when the price of the land was high, for slum clearance and for overspill development. Present subsidies on newly built houses are geared to the current rate of interest. Interest above a rate of 4% per annum is paid by the Exchequer.

Local authorities charge interest and the cost of maintaining the property to their housing account. The income of the account is represented by tenants' rents and Exchequer subsidy, which in 1964 amounted to £94 million. The deficit on the account was £39 million and total subsidies therefore amounted to £133 million.

If all citizens could rent council houses, the subsidy would merely constitute an addition to incomes. This is very far from the the case, the number of people wishing to rent greatly exceeds the accommodation available. People are selected according to housing need and residential qualifications. A family which might be considered by a local authority in a small provincial town might not even be accepted on the waiting list of a large city.[8] Within the same area, selection is very much a matter of chance. Indeed, the Central Housing Advisory Committee in 1949 reported that one authority actually used the ballot box for allocating council housing.[9] Even if a perfect national system of selection were possible, needs would change as the tenants' children grew up and became self-supporting.

TABLE 2

Housing Ownership 1964

		Nos. in '000s	
Local authority		4,739	27%
Rented—Uncontrolled	870		
Controlled	2,873		
Rent free	849		
	——	4,592	27%
Owner-occupied—Bought	3,860		
Being Bought	3,988		
	——	7,848	46%
		17,179	100%

Source: Ministry of Housing and Local Government, Housing Statistics No. 1, 1966.
Note: The Ministry of Labour Family Expenditure Survey records a lower proportion of rent-free and owner-occupied accommodation and a higher proportion of private rented and local authority housing. The split between owner-occupied houses bought and being bought has been made on the basis of the family Expenditure Survey. The estimate for controlled premises is based on Donnison's estimate for July, 1960, and subsequently extrapolated. Donnison, D. V. et al. 'Housing since the Rent Act'. Occasional Paper on Social Administration, No. 3, Codicote Press 1961. Over 10% of the rented accommodation is furnished. (Based on the ratio from the Family Expenditure Survey, 1965.)

Council housing is not always allotted in practice to the poorest families. In 1965, 58% of households in council dwellings had over £20 per week; the figure for unfurnished private rented accommodation was 46%.[10] Council tenants had a larger number of earners per household and this increased household income. Even so in 1962, 29% of heads of household in council houses had incomes of £12 10s. and over per week. Only 24% of the tenants of privately rented accommodation had this income. In 1964 average local authority household incomes in England and Wales were 17% higher than those of privately rented accommodation.[11]

Further, the amount of the subsidy varies enormously from area to area. The exchequer subsidy is paid to the local authority and not to the tenants.[12] Some authorities actually make a 'profit' on the housing account and the amount of subsidy per tenant varies considerably, between local housing authorities. The level of rents depends largely on the proportion of pre-war houses owned by the authority; where most houses are post-war (as in the New Towns), rents are fairly high. The subsidy recorded represents only a fraction of the true subsidy. Present tenants gain from the defects of the method of accounting adopted; pre-war houses are valued in pre-war £s and post-war houses in post-war £s.

Further distortions arise from the various rent reduction or social aid schemes in existence. Some local authorities fix rent as a proportion of income. This is inequitable as ability to pay is not a fixed proportion of income, the magnitude of the income and needs, including the number of children, are important factors.[13] Others make deductions from income in respect of spouse and children and limit rent to the excess of this reduced income above a base figure.

If true economic rents were to be charged they would not be based on the historic cost to local authorities of providing dwellings. In the short run, they are the rents at which existing supply and demand would balance. In the long run, they are based on the contemporary costs of replacing the dwelling in question.[14] In the market the prices of old houses, after allowance for the difference in amenities, bear a fairly constant relationship to those of new houses. The rents of older, vacant, uncontrolled flats are similarly influenced by those of new flats. Accordingly, newcomers to a district or newly married couples not eligible for council housing, pay an effective rent based on replacement value and not historic cost. This rent is much higher than local authority rents, which in 1964 constituted only 7.8% of the average net earnings of an industrial worker with a wife and two children.[15] In 1964 a sample of advertised rents in Willesden, London, were four times as high as average London County Council rents.[16]

It is estimated that the average cost of new local authority dwellings in 1964 was £2,600.[17] Over 55% of the stock of local authority housing was built since the war[18]—a much higher proportion than for any other types of housing. Let us assume that pre-war housing values are discountable by 25% and post-war by 10%—an average of 17%. This is a conservative estimate and considerably higher than the average discount rates quoted by the Co-operative Building Society.'[9] Accordingly the 1964 value of average existing local autho-

51

rity dwellings is £2,158. Interest at $6\frac{3}{4}\%$, plus £28 per annum for maintenance and management, equals £174 per annum.[20] As the mean rent was only £67[21]—the true subsidy is £107, of which £28 is recorded and £79 concealed. This annual subsidy amounts to £507 million—£374 million more than that recorded. A substantial portion of this total subsidy will accrue to the lowest income groups, but a larger amount will also benefit families in the middle income bands; the precise allocation of the benefits depends upon the method by which each individual housing authority determines the level of rent payable.

(ii) *Rent controlled accommodation*

Rents of privately owned accommodation were being gradually decontrolled during the inter-war period. With the outbreak of the war in 1939 controls were reintroduced once again. With some exceptions, rents were controlled at their 1939 levels until the 1957 Rent Act. This Act decontrolled about 400,000 dwellings with a minimum rateable value of £40 in London and Scotland and £30 elsewhere. Further, all dwellings were to be decontrolled on a change of tenacy. Controlled rents could be raised to double the 1939 level. The process of decontrol continues, and substantial numbers of houses previously available for renting are being sold to owner-occupiers. However, it is probable that quite a large stock of controlled housing will be with us for a number of years to come.

It is difficult to estimate the subsidy enjoyed by tenants of rent controlled property. If, on average, the better dwellings (the 36% with unshared baths) are worth 50% of the cost, including land, of the new local authority dwellings, and the remaining 64% are worth 30%, rent controlled property should be let at 45% of local authority economic rents.[22]

It is estimated that average rent was £56[23] per annum. Accordingly, the subsidy amounts to £22 per annum or a total of £63 million. This figure is higher than a conservative estimate of £40 to £50 million trade in 1964.[24] This subsidy is borne by the landlords, but whether past or present it is impossible to determine. Indeed, controls of some form have been with us for so long that most property including controlled tenancies must have been bought or inherited as controlled.

(iii) *Owner-occupied*

As a result of income tax concessions and the shortage of accommodation to let, more and more people have become owner-occupiers. By 1964, 46% of all dwellings were so owned, and this proportion is rising. Income of owner-occupiers is above average—in England and Wales in 1964 owner-occupier households had incomes 40% higher than those of council tenants.[25]

Until Schedule 'A' income tax was abolished in 1963, owner-occupiers paid tax on the 1936/37 imputed rent of their houses. Since 1963 notional rent has escaped tax altogether. Thus, a man who bought a house for £3,000 lives rent-free. Another who invested £3,000 in securities to yield £180 gross per annum, the sum required to pay the rent of an identical house, would be left after tax with only £105. Accordingly, both men have a true annual income of £180 from their investment but one pays tax of £75 and the other pays none.

The average price of all houses mortgaged in 1964 was £3,308.[26] As older houses are not easily mortgageable and as some owner-occupied dwellings are only part of a house, 15% will be deducted from this figure to obtain an estimate of the average value of all owner-occupied houses, £2,812. Interest at $6\frac{3}{4}$% less £34 per annum for maintenance equals £156 per annum per owner-occupied house. This vast notional income amounts to £1,220 million per annum. This figure is over double the Government estimate[27] for imputed rent and arises from the fact that gross values and rateable values are much lower than replacement values. As in the case of rented accommodation, an allowance for depreciation has not been made. Depreciation would reduce the notional income slightly. It is probable that part of this is offset by a rise in real terms in the value of land.

The subsidy can be calculated by multiplying the notional income by the average marginal rate of tax applicable. The average annual income of owner-occupier households in England and Wales was £1,441.[28] After deducting an estimate for members of the household other than husband and wife, average income was £1,290.[29] The addition of notional rent would bring average couples into the standard rate bracket at the margin.

A rate of 31%[30] has been estimated and the subsidy calculated at £378 million, which is very close to the hidden subsidy to local authority tenants of £374 million.[31]

This subsidy is mainly enjoyed by those best able to look after themselves. People with small incomes, many women and the middle aged, in practice find it difficult or impossible to secure mortgages and thus become owner-occupiers. Only about 15% of new mortgagors are aged 45 or over and only 3% are aged 55 or over.[32]

In 1964 mortgagors obtained tax relief on interest of at least £225 million. It is logical that such relief should be granted against notional income. Indeed, this was how the relief first came to be given when imputed rent was taxed in a generous but proper manner prior to the last war. To grant such deductions against income which is no longer taxed is incomprehensible.

(iv) *Conclusion*

People living in local authority, rent controlled and owner-occupied dwellings have a higher true income than that recorded in the Family Expenditure Survey and therefore in the Nicholson/C.S.O. studies.

The total subsidy has been estimated at £948 million, of which all but £63 million is borne by central and local government. Of this sum, only £133 million is recorded, the balance of £815 million is concealed. This figure excludes the benefit which accrues to owner-occupiers from the fact that they are exempt from capital gains tax.[33]

Pensions and Life Assurance

The notional income resulting from the special tax treatment of occupational pensions and life assurance premiums differs from that applying to owner-occupied housing. Instead of extra income accruing to the beneficiary now, an augmented additional income is built up to provide a benefit in the future. The security resulting from this provision is a benefit which members of superannuation schemes enjoy and to the cost of which many contribute. However, part of the contribution is derived from the Exchequer in the form of tax saving. If incomes could be exactly averaged over life, the total tax paid on life income would fall substantially, because marginal rates of tax, especially on high incomes, exceed average rates. The tax rules enable contributors to pension schemes to spread income more evenly over a large part of their adult life and particularly to reduce their taxation liability.

The income foregone is not only the employee's contribution to the pension scheme; it is also that of the employer. Income statistics exclude employer's contribution to pension and life assurance schemes and accordingly the incomes of those benefitting are understated. When comparing the tax burdens of different individuals, this notional income should be added back and tax calculated on income less combined contributions. If everyone benefitted equally, or even proportionately, this benefit could be disregarded. However, large groups are effectively excluded and, therefore, the tax saving on pensions must be taken into account. The problem may be further illustrated by hypothetical examples.

If an employee earning £26 per week pays £1 into a pension scheme and his employer the same, his weekly income is really £27 but he is taxed on £25 only. He thus gets a tax benefit of £32 per annum. In addition, the income earned by the pension fund is

54

exempt from tax. Pensioners are, of course, taxed on the pension benefit.[34] However, income on retirement is likely to be lower than when at work and consequently the tax paid will be less. This is the more so in view of the special tax concessions applicable to retired people. The savings are particularly high when earnings are high. Thus, a man earning £7,000 per annum, with joint contributions of £600, saves surtax and half earned income relief on the premium. When he draws his pension of, say £3,500 he escapes surtax and obtains full earned income relief. This spreading of income over time reduces the progressiveness of taxation.[35] Most of these tax concessions for the employed are also available to the self-employed and many professional and business men are covered. In the Civil Service, retirement age is low and all contributions are paid by the employer. In 1955 the Royal Commission on the Civil Service estimated that pensions cost 18% of actual salaries.

Most pension schemes in the private and public sectors include life cover to protect the employee's family if death occurs before retirement.[36] The amount of cover varies from about £600 upwards and £10,000 is not uncommon. On the one hand, the entire premiums to provide this assurance are exempt from tax; on the other, death benefits paid to estates of beneficiaries are tax free. Ineligible citizens securing similar benefits obtain much smaller tax relief.

In addition to group schemes, many companies provide individual arrangements, 'top hat pensions', for senior executives. The latter effectively give up a portion of their gross salary in return for a pension on retirement. At this highest level of tax, the net cost of an annual premium of £1,000 is only £88. In addition, one quarter of the actuarial value of the combined superannuation and top hat pension can be commuted for a tax free lump sum. High nominal business salaries are often worthwhile only as a base for calculating maximum permissible top hat pensions. In the public sector tax free lump sums on retirement are common.

Group scheme annual premiums amounted to £1,000 million in 1964/5.[37] However, only about one half of the working force are covered. In 1964/65, 42% of annual incomes amounted to £1,000 or over. In that year 54% of employee contributors were in this income bracket and their contributions amounted to 72% of the total.[38] The benefit from favourable taxation policies is therefore concentrated among higher than average income earners to a marked extent.

Pension benefits are now enjoyed by most salaried staff in the public and private sectors and by professional people. At the end of 1967, 75% of male non-manual workers employed by private sector organizations with pension schemes were covered for pensions. The corresponding figure for the public sector was 90%. In all, 4.7 million male non-manual workers were estimated to be covered for occupational pensions.[39] Some, though usually not very generous, provision is also made for a majority of manual workers employed by organizations with occupational schemes. Nevertheless, while 75% of firms with pension schemes employ both manual and non-manual staff, the pension schemes of only 55% of such firms cover both these classes of worker; the manual worker is excluded by a significant number of firms.[40]

Female workers are even more clearly discriminated against; 85% of firms with pension schemes employ both male and female workers but only 50% of their schemes incorporate both sexes. Women are therefore frequently excluded. Over the decade prior to 1967 there was some growth in the proportion of occupational pension scheme members belonging to schemes which provided cover for both manual and non-manual workers. During 1964, the year on which our own estimates are based, it is probably that half male manual employees and the majority of female employees were not earning occupational pension benefits. The differential treatment of these categories of employee arises not only from their frequent exclusion, but also because eligibility requirements are sometimes more stringent and the practice of opting for refunds of contributions on leaving service is more common among female and male manual workers.

Tax relief on life assurance premiums not connected with pension schemes is at the rate of 40%. The first £10 of annual premium is, however, allowed in full. This relief is available for income tax, but not surtax purposes. Annual premiums amounted to approximately £500 million in 1964.[41] At the standard earned income rate of tax the saving is 13%. If the assured's income is below the taxable limit there is, of course, no relief. Indeed, one minority at least, those who are not good medical risks, are excluded from life assurance schemes, but nevertheless contribute to the subsidy enjoyed by their healthy fellow citizens.

This method of saving is used by some owner-occupiers to pay off mortgages and they, therefore, enjoy a further subsidy. It is now being used widely by unit trusts in connection with schemes that are not primarily concerned with assurance.

It is probably that incomes were understated by at least £700 million in 1964 as a result of employers' contributions to pensions, top hat and life assurance schemes.[42] In 1963 employers' contributions to pension schemes alone amounted to £620 million and this had risen to £920 million by 1967.[43] The income of the funds has been estimated at £437 million and the tax saving on this income is £170 million.[44] The total gross subsidy can be calculated as follows : —

	£m.	£m.	
Income tax foregone on pension premiums of	1,000	240	(45)
Income tax foregone on private life assurance premium deductions.	210 ⎫	74	(46)
Income tax foregone on scheme life assurance premium deductions.	100 ⎭		
Income tax foregone on income of pension funds		170	(47)
		£484m.	

To this sum additions should be made for the following.

(a) Public sector notional pension and life assurance premiums; the benefit arises whether or not premiums are actually paid.

(b) The postponement of payment of tax until pensions are drawn constitutes an interest free loan and augments the income of funds.

(c) Tax foregone on the capital appreciation of funds.

A substantial deduction must, of course, be made in respect of the tax borne by pensioners. This tax is, however, normally suffered at a lower rate than would have applied during the working life of the contributor.

If the net subsidy is only equal to the tax saving on the income of the fund and life assurance relief, it amounts to £244 million per annum and this would be a very conservative estimate.

Self-employed Tax Treatment and Capital Gains

In 1964/65 there were 2.1 million assessments of business and professional profits.[48] Of these 73% appertained to individuals, 13% to partnerships and 14% to companies. The estimated number of self-employed was two million—11% of the number of wage and salary earners.[49] Average individual assessment, excluding partnerships and companies, was only £690—£80 less than the average income of male and female wage earners, and £250 less than the average earnings of male industrial manual workers. Of these assessments, 25% were under £250 and 50% under £500 per annum. Actual earned incomes were higher, because some traders had more than one assessment and some had other earned income. In the case of companies, many of which are effectively one or two man businesses, 61% had assessments of under £250 per annum. These, however, were usually made after deducting the salaries of the proprietors and, therefore, actual earned income was higher.

It is difficult to account for the very low average incomes from trades and professions. By their very nature, these incomes are less rigidly accounted for than are wages and salaries.[47] In addition, the income tax rules are more generous in allowing expenses under Schedule 'D' (trades and professions) than they are under Schedule 'E' (wage and salaries). The former need only be wholly and exclusively incurred for the purpose of earning profits. The latter must also be necessarily incurred. The 1955 Royal Commission on Taxation accepted that the two classes of tax-payer were differently treated and even considered giving Schedule 'E' taxpayers a special allowance to rectify their position in relation to the self-employed. It is not possible to estimate with any degree of accuracy the amount of additional income not assessed, but it is probably substantial.

Capital gains are a source of income which has always been omitted from national income statistics. Over the past twenty years, equity prices have risen by an average of 8% per annum. Even allowing for the fall in the value of money, this has, in the past, been a major source of income. Until 1965 long-term gains were untaxed, these are now taxed at concessionary rates. Owner-occupied houses continue, however, tax free. The arbitrary differentiation between capital and revenue profits is a complicating myth. All increases in real values are income spread over time, to the recipient.

In the past few years capital gains have been relatively small and the yield since the introduction of the tax has been negligible. If substantial real gains do occur again the value of the concessionary rates will be considerable.

Conclusions

The scale of these additional incomes and subsidies is so large that, unless they are accounted for, a comparison of nominal income between people is of limited value. Two taxpayers with the same nominal income do not enjoy the same standard of wellbeing if one lives in a comfortable, cheap, subsidized house and the other in dilapidated, high rent accommodation. Similarly, if one enjoys pension benefits and the other does not, real incomes differ from nominal incomes. It was estimated that these subsidies in 1964 amounted to £1,192 million, of which all but £133 million is concealed and all but £63 million provided by government.[48] Further, recorded incomes are understated by an even larger amount, because the subsidy is, in some cases, only the tax omitted on notional incomes. When these huge sums are compared with the total yield of personal income tax, amounting to £3,053 million, it is apparent that they are of great significance. This is the more so, because they benefit specific sections of citizens only, and not necessarily the poorest.

NOTES

1. The use of 1964 data as a basis for our own calculations in Chapter 6 does not prejudice our findings. The C.S.O. studies had acquired a firmly established methodology by this date and our findings are largely unaffected by the small changes that have occurred in the basis data since then. Our aim in making these calculations is merely to indicate the complexity in the patterns of income distribution which even the Nicholson/C.S.O. studies have not revealed. For this reason the choice of a base year and the precise figures involved is not of crucial importance. The crucial factor is this very complexity which

we have tried to emphasize in our calculations and the extent to which the burden of net taxation is affected by whether, for example, family income is augmented by the wife working and whether, or not, the family are owner occupiers.

2. From 1969 employer's contributions are to be treated as indirect taxes falling on intermediate goods and services, within the C.S.O. studies.

3. Report of the Committee of Inquiry into the Impact of Local Rates on Households, (Allen Report), London, HMSO, 1965.

4. The overall effect of graduated contributions is slightly regressive but a flat rate contribution is of course a distinctly regressive type of taxation.

5. Ministry of Labour, Family Expenditure Survey, Report for 1964, London, HMSO.

6. Merrett, A. J. and Monk, D. A. G., 'The Structure of U.K. taxation 1962–63' in the Bulletin of the Oxford University Institute of Economic and Statistics, August, 1966.

7. As we have noted, from 1969 onwards the C.S.O. are adapting their procedures to give recognition to this possibility.

8. Cullingworth, J. B., 'Housing and Local Government', London, Allen & Unwin, 1966.

9. For further references to the problem of council house allocation see the Report of the Committee on Housing in Greater London (Milner Holland), Cmnd. 2605, London, HMSO, 1965.

10. Family Expenditure Survey, 1965 and see the Milner Holland Report, op. cit.

11. Allen Report, op. cit.

12. See Nevitt, A. A. 'Housing, Taxation and Subsidies", London, Nelson, 1966, for a detailed account of the deficiencies of this mode of subsidizing housing.

13. See Parker, R., 'The Rents of Council Houses', Occasional Paper on Social Administration, No. 22, London, Bell, 1967.

14. Hemming, M. F. W., 'Price of Accommodation' National Institute Economic Review, August 1964.

15. After deducting employees' National Insurance contributions and income tax and adding family allowances.

16. Milner Holland Report, op. cit.

17. Based on Ministry of Housing Statistics No. 5, 1967, for new tenders for three-bedroom houses. A conservative addition has been made for land. In 1963 average cost of land for dwellings in London was £1,150. (Report of the L.C.C. Housng and Finance Committee, 1964).

18. Allen Report, op. cit.

19. Co-operative Building Society, Occasional Bulletin, 1965.

20. Allowance should be made for depreciation in real terms, this would raise the subsidy further. Depreciation is partly offset by probable rises in real land values.

21. Ministry of Housing and Local Government, Housing Statistics, No. 4, January 1967.

22. In London in 1960 only 36% of privately rented dwellings had an unshared bath, as against 91% of local authority dwellings. Only 58% had an unshared W.C. as against 92% for council dwellings. Milner Holland Report, op. cit.

23. As most occupiers of rent controlled housing had household incomes of under £15 per weeks average rent of unfurnished accommodation as a ratio of local authority rents for households with under £15 per week was calculated. The proportion, based on the Family Expenditure Survey for 1965, was 78%. (These figures are not available for 1964.) A slightly higher ratio, 83% was used to allow for families with higher incomes living in rent controlled housing. The mean net local authority rent of £67 was multiplied by 83% to obtain the estimate of £56. This estimate is probably on the high side, because the Milner Holland Report stated that average rent for single occupancy controlled houses in London was only £71. London rents are higher than elsewhere and multiple occupancy dwellings are cheaper.

24. Kaim-Caudle, P. R., 'A New Look at Housing Subsidies', Local Government Finance, March 1964.

25. Allen Report., op. cit.

26. Calculated from the Ministry of Housing statistics, No. 3, 1966.

27. Central Statistical Office, National Income and Expenditure Blue Book for 1965, London HMSO.

28. Allen Report op. cit.

29. Income of members other than husbands and wives amounted to 16.8% of household incomes according to the Family Expenditure Survey, 1965. This proportion has been used.

30. An average of standard rate, standard rate less earned income relief, highest reduced rate and highest reduced rate less earned income relief. This is the same as the Building Society Composite rate in 1965. The reduction for earned income relief has been made to compensate mortgagors with earned incomes only who lose this relief in interest payments.

31. The incidence of the subsidy to owner occupiers is such that benefits vary in inverse ratio to income, the higher the income, the higher the subsidy. Thus, if an owner-occupier'was in the top surtax bracket, the £156 tax-free notional income in 1964 was equivalent to a subsidy of £138. If his income was below the income tax limit, the subsidy was nil. The relief to mortgagors who pay little tax and benefit from the new mortgage option scheme extends the anomaly further because they benefit from a lower, though substantial subsidy.

32. Ministry of Housing Statistics No. 3, 1966.

33. If house prices rise annually by as little as 2% and average capital gains tax chargeable is only 10%, the subsidy on the total stock of housing is £48 million per annum.

34. A few schemes provide only life assurance rate relief for employees' contributions, but the benefits on retirement are untaxed.

35. For a fuller discussion, see Titmuss, R. M., 1962, op. cit.

36. The Government Actuary (1968) estimated that 90% of members of private sector pension schemes receive cover which includes the payment of some benefit in the event of death during service. This benefit is not necessarily provided at a generous level and some 20% of members are only covered for the return of their own contributions. All public sector pensions provide some such coverage and 19% of men are now in schemes providing widow's pension,the corresponding figure in private sector schemes is 30%, Government Actuary's Department, 'Occupational pension schemes: third Survey', London HMSO 1968.

37. Report of the Annual Conference of the Association of Superannuation Funds, 1965.

38. 109th Report of the Commissioners of Inland Revenue.

39. The figures in this paragraph are taken from the Government Actuary's Third Survey of Occupational Schemes, op. cit.

40. ibid., p. 9.

41. 109th Report of the Commissioners of Inland Revenue, London HMSO.

42. In his 'Principles of Pension Fund Investment', W. G. Nursaw, London, (Hutchinson, 1966), estimated that two-thirds of pension premiums were paid by employers. We have used the lower figure of 60%. Associated life assurance and top hat premiums have been estimated at £100 million.

43. Government Actuary's Third Survey, op. cit. Table 7.

44. Nurshaw, W. G., op. cit. Value of Pension Funds in 1964:

Self-administered	£5,007 million
Life Assurance Schemes	£2,500 million
	£7,507 million

If the yield on life assurance schemes (mainly with profits) is 5½ % and 6% on others, the total annual income is £437 million.

45. Building Society composite rate less earned income relief has been used.

46. 109th Report of the Commissioners of Inland Revenue,

47. £437 million at standard rate of income tax.

48. 109th Report of the Commissioners of Inland Revenue, op. ct.

49. The folowing assumptions have been made:-

(a) Individuals equal 85% of individual assessments.

(b) There are 2.35 individuals per partnership and a deduction of 15% has been made.

(c) Companies with assessments of under £2,000 per annum are owned by the self-employed. A deduction, as above, of 15% has been made.

50. An article in the Times, dated 10th April, 1967, by four City executives, stated for example, that 'evasion has, in fact been fairly widespread in this country since income tax was introduced, particularly among casual workers, the self-employed and small businessmen. The great majority of tax evaders in Britain today probably belong to these classes.'

51. This excludes benefits which results from self-employed tax treatment.

5. THE ALLOCATION OF BENEFITS

Despite our numerous and detailed criticisms of the studies referred to in the last chapter, the most important source of imprecision in estimates of redistribution has as yet received little attention.

After deducting taxation from household income, Nicholson allocated imputed values of welfare benefits to households; he distributed the cost to the Government of providing these services to families who were known, or assumed, to have used them. This process introduces many possible sources of error for both technical and theoretical reasons. Nicholson, it must be readily admitted, makes the very best of a difficult situation; nevertheless it remains true to say that the theoretical problems of making such an allocation have been virtually ignored. In considering the theoretical justification (if any) for this process, we shall be referring back more explicitly than in the preceeding sections to the preoccupation of the first chapter—the raison d'etre of the welfare state and the relationship of redistribution studies to the discussion of social policies. We will also be considering the actual procedures adopted by Nicholson in allocating benefits and noting the technical limitations within which he had to work.

Allocated Indirect Benefits

Food Subsidies

Food subsidies accruing to the consumer, Nicholson suggests, were equal to most if not all of the total food subsidy in 1953 when rationing was still in operation for basic foods. By the late nineteen fifties (1957 and 1959) consumer benefits were assumed to be negligible and no attempt has been made to allocate them to consumers since 1953. Only the remaining milk subsidy was allocated to consumers in 1957; all other agriculture subsidies which were known to be received by individual farmers were included in their initial income. It should be noted in this context that Cartter allocated £387m. in

61

food subsidies to consumers in 1948/49 and a further £47m. in agricultural payments to farmers; the change in redistribution resulting from the changes in these subsidies alone was of considerable importance between 1948/49 in 1957-59. Especially is this so since by far the greater proportion of both was imputed to incomes of £500 per annum or less in Cartter's study. The distribution of these subsidies and the amounts involved are mentioned not in order to question the assumptions on which the allocations were made, but rather to indicate the extent to which the decline in food subsidies and the differing treatment of them by the different researchers, may have influenced the total picture of income redistribution over the period. Food subsidies alone amounted to only a little less than one quarter of all divisible benefits in 1948-49 and they were the largest single divisible benefit allocated—about £50m. more than pensions.

Housing Subsidies

Three kinds of housing subsidy could have been considered as benefits: those accruing to tenants of rent controlled properties; to local authority tenants; and to owner occupiers.

The redistribution of income from landlords to tenants in controlled tenancies has been recognized as being of importance by Nicholson, but has not been quantified. The Family Expenditure Survey provided data on which tenants occupied controlled lettings, but little study of this aspect of rent control had been undertaken at the time of Nicholson's earlier studies. The task of making an assessment, ab initio, of the transfer occurring, would not have been commensurate with the information gained. It will be clear that this source of redistribution, while contained within the broad concept of social policy that we have discussed, is quite alien to the more limited public finance orientation of Barna and Cartter. It is for this reason that the brief reference which Nicholson made to this problem has been noted here.[1] However, Nicholson has not departed from the practice adopted by the earlier researchers.

In dealing with Local Authority housing, data on the total sum of distributed subsidies could be coupled with the existence of a council tenancy as determined by the Family Expenditure Survey. The average subsidy per local authority dwelling was allocated to such tenants. As this was the national average subsidy no allowance is made for variations between local authorities. The exclusion of differential and rent rebate schemes introduces an element of error tending, one assumes to produce an underestimate of the amount of redistribution actually effected by these subsidies. This source of error is not likely to be very large relative to the study as a whole, but it is a real deficiency and is one of the few sources of bias which may produce an under, rather than an over, estimate of the egalitarian effects of income redistribution.[2] Subsidies benefiting owner occupiers were discussed in detail in Chapter 4.

Allocated Direct Benefits

Having reviewed the allocation of what Nicholson terms indirect benefits, we are left with what is perhaps the most interesting aspect of a redistribution study for the student of social policy, namely the allocation of the imputed values of direct benefits.

For Nicholson the transfer incomes; family allowances, national insurance benefits and non-contributory pensions with the addition of national assistance grants; presented no insurmountable, practical difficulties. Information was available from respondents on which of these benefits they received; obviating the kind of assumptions which Cartter and Barna found necessary.

Benefits from the National Health Service are allocated in a similar way in both Nicholson's and Cartter's study to age groups according to their estimated differential need of the services provided. Nicholson, in the absence of information on adults' ages, weighted the benefits imputed to households receiving retirement and old age pensions in order to allow for the greater needs of this age group. However, the allowance made is for variations in need, which bear no known relationship to variations in the utilization of services by different groups, or the quality of benefit obtained. Equally, no attempt is made to quantify variations in utilization and the quality of service received by reference to *other* variables such as socio-economic class.

Nicholson's access to the Family Expenditure Survey data on the distribution of children by age among families of different income groups and composition, made it possible to allocate educational benefits to these groups in the light of the type of education being received by each child. In 1953 and 1957 the average public expenditure (on current account) per child in all grant aided and maintained schools, was attributed to each child of school age. This method clearly failed to differentiate between the quality and, therefore, the monetary equivalent of the benefit (considering education as a purely consumption good at present) accruing to pupils at different types of school. Before 1959 Nicholson's approach was superior to Cartter's only in so far as his source data on the distribution of children by income range was less subject to bias than Cartter's estimate.[3]

In view of this, Nicholson's allocation of benefits was not necessarily more useful in the two earlier studies than it was in Cartter's analysis. However, within the confines of sample bias the method of allocation used since 1959 represents a considerable methodological improvement. For example, one source of bias to be found in the allocations of 1953 and 1957, but not 1959, was the neglect of children receiving education after the statutory school leaving age. Since the terminal age of formal education is correlated with income, an inaccurate allocation of benefit occurred during the early years of the study even when one ignores the qualitative difference between the types of school attended.

For the 1959 estimate Nicholson attributed the expenditure per child by public authorities on primary education to children in this age range and made a distinction between secondary modern and grammar (including technical) schools for those children reported to be attending these two groups of schools. The proportion of public expenditure imputed to pupils of grammar, as opposed to secondary modern, schools was determined by reference to the number of teachers employed in each type of school. The average public expenditure on all grant aided schools was attributed to families containing pupils of independent schools.

The use of the number of teachers to estimate the benefits accruing to pupils of each form of education is a very arbitrary means of refining the allocation. Quite apart from the investment potential (for the individual) of a grammar school education, the purely consumption good aspects of education may be expected to vary considerably between different types of school and these are not reflected in the statistical allocation of benefits. Nicholson's assumption seems to be more appropriate to a quantification of the intent of educational policy than to its achievements. If this is acceptable within a public finance orientation to redistribution (and it is not suggested that it is acceptable to Nicholson except in the short term), it has been argued in this book that such procedures may be positively harmful to the discussion of social policy.

From what has been said above with regard to secondary education benefits, it will be seen that basing the allocation of benefits from university and technical college education on the public expenditure absorbed by these sectors is open to criticism. Though allocating these benefits on this basis is an improvement over having to omit them altogether, as was the case in 1953. Nicholson was not able to allocate benefits arising from teacher training in earlier years, but this difficulty was overcome in 1963. In the same year students in C.A.Ts. were also treated separately for the first time. To the extent that these student differ from those in universities in terms of parental (or more precisely household) incomes and the composition of their family of origin, a biased estimate will have been made of the distribution of higher and further education benefits prior to 1963.

The purpose of this section on the allocation of benefits is to examine the advances in methodology which Nicholson's work contains, to discuss some of the difficulties arising from the procedures adopted in the allocation of benefits and, finally, to indicate some of the many hindrances to comparability between the three researchers' work, and within Nicholson's work, between the different years for which data are available. This third aim has not been discussed explicitly and therefore warrants a brief consideration at this point.

Each of the refinements to the allocation process that we have mentioned, present their attendent difficulties for the comparability of results. In the case of Nicholson's work the analysis of 1953 is most difficult to compare with later work in terms of techniques. For a branch of research needing and gaining refinement fairly rapidly in the early stages of its development, ensuring comparability may seem to be of marginal importance. Nevertheless, since such measurements are likely to be used to indicate changes in redistribution over time and are most immediately relevant to social policy in such a context, alternative sets of data based on the various assumptions employed are required.

Nicholson provides such an alternative assessment for 1959 on 1953 assumptions and also adjusts the 1959 results to more closely parallel Barna's procedures for 1937. Both these attempts to improve comparability are referred to later, at present it need only be stressed that the latter does not in any way make the basic studies more comparable in themselves. As Nicholson mentions, the results need to be interpreted with great caution. Despite the loss of validity in the figures for the later year, the former adjustment is most useful in permitting some comparisons to be made throughout the period of the fifties. The later studies have included few important changes in methodology and results are broadly comparable from 1959 and throughout the sixties.

The Theoretical Problems of Allocating Benefits

In allocating both taxes and benefits, redistribution studies have averaged the individual experiences of each household within a given income range to arrive at some notion of the net loss or benefit experienced by the income group as a whole. This is in many senses an unsatisfactory procedure, per se, but some such form of averaging is necessary if a study is to move beyond the description of the experiences of individual families. The use of income groups for this purpose is the most practical way of attempting to isolate, statistically, the relationship between redistribution and the distribution of life chances between different 'classes' of people. (Though it cannot be

65

said that the income ranges have been related in any meaningful way with the concept of social class).

Necessary as this use of income groups is, it is a misleading device and especially so in relation to the distribution of welfare benefits. For though the relationship is complex and sometimes tenuous, taxation is related to the income and expenditure of households; the problem is to discover the kind of relationship which exists. In contrast with taxes, benefits cannot be assumed to be distributed in a way which is related to the distribution of income. While an intention to level up life chances has been imputed to much social policy, the existence of this effect in practice is precisely what is in question.

Averaging the taxation paid by families brings anomalies, indirect taxation in particular varies with the type of housing occupied and goods and services purchased and these factors are not necessarily related to income and family size. In addition direct taxes also vary as a result of factors other than the two which are used to classify families into groups.[4] Nevertheless, if groups identified by income and family size are recognized as containing sub-groups identified by the major factors determining tax payment, the averaging of taxation across income groups is not too misleading. In contrast the receipt of benefits varies in response to a very large number of factors and averaging benefits across income groups yields a statistical picture which is less meaningful than that for direct taxation. There cannot be any presumption as to the distribution of benefits between the households within a single income group (classification by family size as well as income reduces, but does not eliminate the difficulty). The difference in the resources of non-benefit receiving households and those who utilize welfare services may be more pronounced, therefore, than between households who bear above and below average rates of taxation for their family size and income group.

Nicholson justified his procedure of imputing a presumed benefit to all families in an income group (that is to say he justified the imputing of benefits actually received by households, to the income group as a whole) in terms of the 'sense of security' accruing to persons entitled to benefits, whether or not they required them in any one year. The sense of security he suggested, varies with a household's expectation of needing the benefit, which expectation is governed by the experience of households in similar circumstances.[5] Thus he argues that it is possible to impute benefits to all families within a given group (homogeneous with respect to 'circumstance'), by reference to the empirically obtained patterns of receipts enjoyed by members of that group.

This assumption requires further examination, for several problems arise from it for our conceptual approach to redistribution. Firstly, it is likely that a person's (and to some extent a household's) subjective benefit (as in the 'sense of security') will vary with individual experience. The experience of similar households is not the sole determinant of the subjective benefit, unless the group of similar households is homogeneous with respect to all significant variables. Nicholson in fact only holds income range and family composition constant, as we have seen.

The significant variables concerned would be very diverse if a rigorous analysis were attempted. However, two important ones may be mentioned, the first being the variation in the *perception* of a benefit which might be expected to accrue as the result of a given contingency. We have noted that little detailed knowledge exists of the differential utilization by social groups of the services available. No information exists, however, with regard to the variation in the perception of potential benefits. It may be expected that different individuals and households will both over and under estimate the security provided them by social services. In addition to this factor it would be necessary to make allowance for differential perceptions of the seriousness of a contingency, quite apart from the objective criteria of its likelihood of arising to which Nicholson makes reference.

It may further be noted that the 'sense of security' has been 'purchased' at different historical moments by different social groups and with respect to different contingencies. In a study based on the benefits accruing to persons within a single year, it would be necessary to consider the variation in the sense of security resulting from the length of time that the benefit has been available and has been perceived as available. Similar considerations would arise in a longitudinal study. As Peacock and Shannon note 'the C.S.O. study is really offering us a judgement of value to guide allocation of benefit and not simply a statistical technique'.[6]

Nicholson's 'justification' is therefore, both too elaborate and also oversimplified for the nature of the study in hand. It would seem appropriate to use the present reasoning and be far more rigorous and therefore sophisticated, in the classification of households; or, to simply state the procedure to be adopted without attempting such justification. When the object of a policy is to provide a benefit to all persons who may require it, any evaluation of this process in terms of the vertical redistribution effected between income groups is too unsophisticated a measure to reflect the operation of the services qua services, (i.e. their contingency redistribution function). To attempt to introduce such refinement into a method of quantification designed for the limited purpose of measuring inequality seems unnecessary. To adopt this averaging procedure unashamedly for a specific purpose is most defensible, however, if its limitations are spelled out and alternative, complimentary measures are developed wherever possible. In this respect separate research on specific groups (i.e. large families) would be a useful addition to the present kind of study.

Having said that benefits should be thought of only in monetary terms and averaged without reservation across income groups, it must be added that this only applies where benefits are available to all members of the income group and the non-use of them in a particular year depends solely on the non-occurrence of the contingency for which they are provided. Where, on the other hand, the contingency does arise but the benefit is not claimed due to the ability and preference of the household concerned to meet the need privately, there seems to be an a priori case for not imputing the benefits to the household. Most noticeably does this situation arise in education where some households with children of school age choose not to submit a claim against the State system. To allocate to them, as Nicholson does, the value of the publicly financed education the child could be receiving is to overwork the concept of security, at least in so far as a single year of observation and accountancy is used. In a number of such cases the sense of security provided by the State system may be considerable at some time during the private education of the child, in others this subjective benefit may never be experienced. It is not likely that a constant benefit, equal to that gained by children actually obtaining a State financed education, accrues to even the majority of households whose children are educated in the private sector. If a study is limited, therefore, to a monetary equivalent of tangible benefits (since these are largely within our competence to quantify while subjective aspects are not) Nicholson's procedure of allocating benefits where the option to use them is not taken up, is misleading.

Equally in the case of the National Health Service a finer analysis of the use made of particular services by persons able to purchase some private medical care, is merited. This is, however, a matter of knowing fairly precisely the pattern of actual use made of the N.H.S. by different clients. Such information is not available.[7] If it became available there would seem to be no reason for allocating the full benefit per person of the N.H.S. as a whole, to those individuals and households purchasing some medical services privately.

A corollary must be added to the above proposition—persons unable or unwilling to benefit fully from the services nominally available to them for reasons other than the purchase of private provision, should also be allocated a reduced or zero monetary equivalent of benefit. This may seem anomolous at first since the elements introduced in such a process are similar in their subjectivity to those to which objection has just been made. In fact the objection was to the treatment of subjective benefits as if they were tangible ones which could be valued in money terms. In this latter case the subjective considerations, particularly pride, ignorance and interpersonal interactions, serve to reduce or nullify the tangible benefits of services which are nominally available to the person at a given standard or quality. It is in this second situation that the paucity of information on the differential benefit gained from, and use made of, social services is most damaging.

While the private purchase of services is cited as sufficient reason for not allocating benefits from state services, indirect state subsidies to the private sector should be included. For example, benefits which independent schools obtain from their charitable status should be allocated to the purchasers of private education. As we have previously seen, however, such forms of redistribution have not yet appeared in their role as social welfare benefits in any study of income inequality.

In all redistribution studies the monetary equivalent of benefit is based on the public expenditure incurred in providing the services. It is very convenient to use public expenditure as a valuation of the benefits produced, but this procedure has many disadvantages. The price mechanism is the only relatively simple means of assigning a monetary value to a good or service consumed by a large number of people. In the absence of the price mechanism there is no means by which to assess people's preferences for particular commodities. The cost of producing them is a rather unsatisfactory, non-market tested, alternative.[8] Nevertheless, it is accepted here not simply because of the difficulty of providing practical alternatives, but also in view of the manifest imperfections in the market situation.

At the very least it may be argued that the non-pricing of 'externalities' in the market could introduce inaccuracies as imponderable in the quantitative sense, as those which public financing and provision may produce in our present measurement of redistribution. Peacock and Shannon argue that in the case of education the prices charged for private education and not public expediture, might be used as a basis for evaluating benefits.[9] Such surrogate measures of the value of social welfare outputs would be of interest, but they cannot be produced with confidence in a predominantly state financed welfare system. Education is almost the only area of benefit in which there is a substantial private sector (in the case of housing the private sector is predominant and we produced estimates of the true value of council house subsidies in the last chapter, with the aid of some data drawn from this sector). The use of surrogate measures of benefit would not overcome the problem of taking 'externalities' into account.

The existence of divergence in the net private and social gain from welfare expenditure also impinges, however, upon the use of public expenditure as a measure of the value of welfare benefits. In so far as education, for example, is an investment for the individual and the society as a whole, the present use of public expenditure in estimating benefits is unsatisfactory. The line of reasoning adopted by the Robbins Report and the authors of studies quoted therein suggests a sufficiently large personal investment element in higher education and therefore in the preliminary, qualifying stages of secondary education, to make the Nicholson allocation look extremely suspect.[10] If we confine ourselves to allocating benefit by reference to public expenditure and therefore to material benefits only, the allocation of benefits on the basis of numbers of teachers is far less acceptable if the investment and not just the consumption aspects of education are borne in mind.

An estimate of the income generated by different types of education would provide a more realistic means of allocating public expenditure to the pupils of different schools. Unfortunately the type of education received and the average life-time income of a person are not simply correlated. Innate ability differences and cultural factors would be expected to give rise to some occupational mobility and divergence in life time earnings, if formal education was held constant.

If such a method was found to be feasible for educational benefits a similar procedure might seem necessary, or more valid than the present one, in the field of health benefits. The investments of health services is even more controversial than that of education, but there can be no doubt that for some persons there is a financial benefit from medical care. The problem of the investment potential of health services at a national level does not immediately concern us. Nevertheless, the empirical difficulties of measuring the different long term returns from health care enjoyed by each section of the population prevents the suggestion being of practical importance.

Complimentary to the need to consider the distribution of income over a longer time span is the possibility, in the cases just mentioned, of computing the cumulative effect of redistributive policies over time for different groups of individuals. In both health and education the value over time of benefits would seem to be directly related to income levels, due to the operation of the benefits in generating and preserving these income levels. Educational benefits in particular present something of a paradox, in that they may be expected to both preserve existing income differentials in general and yet be key factors in the social mobility of particular individuals. This cumulative approach to the study of redistribution cannot easily be pursued, but an indication of the value of the method to social policy may be useful. Cohort analyses, for example, rather than annual studies of redistribution would clearly assist in the type of problem with which Robbins was confronted, namely, the implications of the investment element in education benefits for the financing of university education.[11]

The benefits arising from University and Technical College education were first allocated in 1957. The value of these benefits has been estimated from the level of public expenditure on these services. As in the case of secondary education this system of valuation is unsatisfactory because of the 'investment' value of benefits.

Two basic methods could be used to reflect the investment effect of social service benefits.[12] The first has been mentioned in relation to secondary education. It involves the statistical reallocation of public expenditure between similar kinds of services (different types of secondary schooling or higher education) and the estimation of benefits on the basis of these adjusted figures for public expenditure on each service. This reallocation of public expenditure would be based upon the comparative 'investment' effects of each of the group of services. The total level of public expenditure on a group of services would still determine the valuation of benefits, but the valuation of each benefit would reflect its importance in generating future returns to the recipient (i.e. its investment effect). This method accords with the public expenditure basis of valuation currently employed in the Nicholson/C.S.O. studies. It merely involves a statistical reallocation of total public expenditure.

On the other hand, a more substantial departure could be made from the existing public expenditure approach. Actual public expenditure could be multiplied by a factor which represented the long term income generating effect of the benefit. An average 'multiplier' could be applied to aggregate expenditure on a service (say university education) and the expanded total of public expenditure allocated equally between all recipients. Alternatively, with more detailed information on the investment effects of benefits, an individualized 'multiplier' could be applied to the public cost of providing the service received by each social service client. This would entail a radical departure from the existing method of evaluation.

It may reasonably be argued that it would be ludicrous to devise a new method of valuating one or two benefits in isolation. To reflect the investment value, if any, of *all* social service benefits would be more logical. It would also be quite impossible for purely

71

technical reasons. Moreover, it would be unrealistic to attempt complex refinements at a time when even rudimentary information is lacking on the actual use made of some social services. To create wide discrepancies in the sophistication with which each benefit is allocated would not be desirable. The priority in improving methodology lies with the mitigation of the worst defects in our knowledge on the utilization of, for example, the health services.

There are two reasons for having mentioned the investment effects of social service benefits. Firstly, it emphasizes the general point that there are theoretical issues in the allocation of benefit which have received little attention. The validity of redistribution studies rests to a large extent upon the way in which these problems are dealth with in practice. Secondly, the particular issue in question has not been discussed in the existing studies of redistribution.

The methods of valuing social service benefits suggested above are not practicable. They cannot be used to refine the Nicholson/ C.S.O. allocation of benefits; the uncertainties concerning the investment effect of benefits are too great to permit this. The use of a 'multiplier' would greatly magnify any errors in the basic allocation procedure. Nevertheless, the existing method of valuation and allocation cannot be appraised without considering its theoretical implications. Our main concern has been to emphasize that all social service benefits are presently treated as consumption goods. The investment effect of some services is important. The studies of redistribution almost certainly over-estimate the egalitarian effects of social policy by ignoring these investment effects.

To summarize our arguments; we have noted several theoretical problems in the allocation of welfare benefits. The use of governmental expenditure as a basis for quantifying welfare benefits can be criticized on economic and socio-psychological grounds, but the need to limit this valuation to the development of monetary equivalents of notional, objective benefits, is undeniable. Accepting such limitations on the ground of expediency does not rule out the possibility of changing the method of allocating the sum of governmental expenditure, as suggested in relation to education. Equally the public expenditure devoted to individuals (for example in higher education) could be multiplied by a constant representing the estimated investment value of this expenditure to the indivdual. The resulting figure would provide a very tentative indication of the function of such benefits in initiating redistribution over time and not merely during a very short period of time. It must be admitted that these procedures are open to much criticism, but they serve the purpose of emphasizing the need for caution in using the findings of redistribution studies. A study based on a single year and not on longitudinal analyses (of differing life experiences in regard to taxation and benefit) cannot avoid presenting an oversimplification of the impact of welfare benefits on life chances. A study which treats all social service benefits purely as consumer goods has the same deficiencies.

Indeed, we would argue that the vulnerability of Nicholson's estimates may be most convincingly illustrated by considering the redistributive role of direct benefits. These benefits produce the greatest reduction in estimated inequality for families with children and have a significantly greater egalitarian impact for some family types than does income tax and surtax combined. But we have stressed that the distribution of these benefits is virtually an unknown factor. Allocating monetary equivalents of benefit is an extremely uncertain process at present and in attempting to overcome this problem Nicholson probably allocates benefits more in accordance with the broad intentions of social policy than with the reality of social service utilization. The fragile nature of the estimates is most clearly reflected by the treatment accorded to the benefits of higher education. These services probably have by far the most significant 'investment' value for the consumer, of all social services.

Increasing the allocated benefits by several times (through the application of a multiplier to public expenditure on higher education) could obviously and drastically reduce the egalitarian impact of all direct benefits.

The necessity of computing the incidence of welfare benefits by income group is undeniable, but it is a procedure which can only be used at some cost to the sensitivity of the study. Disclosed benefits, council housing for example, are allocated to the income groups of households receiving them. It must therefore be remembered that a household in the income range £816—£988 (1964) living in high rent, poor quality private accommodation is deemed to enjoy the benefit of the average disclosed council house subsidy applicable to that income range. This distortion, together with the fact that large concealed benefits are enjoyed by substantial numbers of families, makes the allocation of benefits to income ranges haphazard. Nicholson's intention was to provide an analysis of redistribution by income groups and for many reasons the further classification of data by family composition produces the most sophisticated analysis that can be reasonably expected. The introduction of further variables such as the sector of the housing market that the family's dwelling falls within, would greatly complicate the presentations of results.

There is therefore a very strong argument for developing income redistribution measures for 'model families', which may be used in conjunction with the holistic type of study which Nicholson has developed. By constructing 'model families' and varying factors such

73

as ages of children and the type of accommodation occupied it would be possible to illustrate the variations in benefits received and taxes paid that occur within Nicholson's income groups. Our calculations in the next chapter are based on a very limited number of such variables, but the value of computing the impact of taxes and benefits (our calculations are limited almost exclusively to taxes) on, for example, council house families and owner occupier families in various income ranges, is very real.

Benefits not allocated by Nicholson

Similar difficulties to those discussed above would arise (though in a more acute form) if the benefits from various social services now grouped in the unallocable class, were imputed to households. While the magnitude of the task of making such an allocation is an understandable deterrent, it is advisable to note the services which are thus excluded from the calculation so that we may gain a more accurate idea of the section of social policy which is represented in the allocation process.

Local authority welfare services are excluded (school meals, milk and welfare foods are the only welfare benefits included), as is legal aid; the benefits arising from both of which could be assessed, by household, with adjustments in the Family Expenditure Survey questionnaire and sample. The same could not be said of the Child Care Service, for example. Any attempt to allocate all the benefits accruing from this service would of necessity involve arbitrary judgments of doubtful validity, at least at this stage in the measurement of success in social casework. Some benefits provided by this service could be allocated despite the difficulty of assessing the effects of social case work. Short term care of children by the local authorities and the provision of cash assistance could both be allocated without much difficulty from the theoretical standpoint.

The predominantly therapeutic services in the penal system, probation and after care, juvenile liaison schemes, training and treatment in penal institutions, might seem to be reasonably allocable. But in addition to the problem of assessing the success of therapy, there is a further complication, for unlike other social work services the penal system must be presumed to bring considerable material benefits to individual persons (as opposed to the society in general) other than its clientele. Potential victims of crime who escape harm or suffer only reduced injury due to the presence of the system of justice (of which these particular services are an integral part) should be considered to be beneficiaries. Even if the efficacy of the system in these matters were not such a source of controversy, allocating benefits between criminals, potential criminals, and other members of society, would be a theoretical and practical task of immense complexity. This is not to say that the services mentioned can be allocated to the category of indivisible benefits without reservation.

It is difficult to assess the effect of excluding these benefits from the allocation process. Some benefits do not accrue to specific individuals and can legitimately be treated as indivisible benefits (much of the expenditure on the penal system falls within this category). The treatment to be accorded to indivisible benefits is discussed below. On the other hand those examples mentioned above suggest that errors could arise from treating them as indivisible benefits. The major benefits (especially from local authority welfare and social work services) are likely to accrue to low and middle income families; excluding them leads to an underestimate of vertical income redistribution. The non-allocation of these benefits (and the neglect of local authority rent rebate schemes mentioned in chapter four) is one of the few factors which might produce an overestimate of inequality.

Fiscal Benefits

The effects of fiscal subsidies are reflected in existing studies of redistribution through the deduction of taxation. The levels of taxation recorded in the Nicholson/C.S.O. studies represent actual tax payments and not the notional taxation liability of families if tax allowances were assumed not to exist. The impact of fiscal subsidies on the distribution of incomes is therefore included in these studies. The progressiveness of income tax and surtax is considerably reduced (though the distribution of income per capita is more equitable in middle and upper income groups) as a result of, for example, child tax allowances.

Nevertheless, it was stressed in chapter two that tax concessions should be seen to be a form of social welfare provision. Though covert in their role as benefits, they give recognition to a range of social needs (the existence of dependents and the purchase of housing or income during future contingencies through insurance, for example). The desire to avoid greater complexity in our fiscal system reinforces the distinction made between social welfare considerations and the pursuit of equity between tax payers within the tax system. But the distinction can only be defended as an administrative one. Viewed from a social policy standpoint, fiscal subsidies are a substantial part of the recognition of need. This fact was partially reflected in the treatment of the 1968 increases in family allowances[13] and the debate on child poverty has concentrated attention on the need to treat the different sectors of social welfare provision logically, as a unitary system.

One of the proposed measures for reducing poverty which has received considerable attention in recent years, the concept of a negative income tax, illustrates the tenuous nature of any distinction between social welfare benefits and fiscal benefits.[14] If Family Allowances were to be replaced by extending the effect of child tax allowances downwards into the non-tax paying income groups, a parallel system of cash payments and tax concessions would operate through the fiscal system. The present treatment of benefits in income redistribution studies would result in the cash payments being represented as benefits, but the tax allowances would only be reflected in the actual as opposed to the notional tax liability of families. A study of redistribution designed to meet the needs of social policy would ideally treat tax concessions of this kind as subsidies and not allow their status as welfare 'payments' to remain concealed.

This could be done by deducting the tax to which families would be *notionally* liable (if these subsidies did not exist) and allocating the subsidies involved as direct benefits. The traditional form of accounting reveals the pattern of income inequality remaining after actual tax payments have been deducted, the proposed method of accounting would present fiscal subsidies *as subsidies* and facilitate an appreciation of the total web of social recognition accorded to social needs. To view social policy in its entirety is an increasingly important need with the growth of complexity and of detailed planning in social welfare provision.[15] Income redistribution studies would be more valuable in social policy discussions if both methods of accounting were utilized and alternative sets of data were produced.

The allocation of Indivisible Benefits

Indivisible benefits generally may be presumed to accrue to some or all members of society and to make no allocation of them, as does Nicholson, is to invite the user of the statistics to make assumptions about the likely beneficiaries. In this circumstance the assumptions employed are less likely to have been formulated after rigorous scrutiny of the alternatives than they would have been if the researchers had allocated these benefits. We have seen that non-allocated social services are not to be assumed to benefit persons in any simply determined way. This is especially true of the important branch of unallocated services which provide various forms of residential care and treatment.

Barna discusses the theoretical question of how these indivisibles may be allocated on arbitrary criteria which nonetheless may be seen to 'appeal to principles of ethics and politics'.[16] Three possible means of allocation are proposed, firstly, in proportion to each unit's income in which case the benefit is estimated, in the case of Barna's own study, to be approximately 10.6% of each unit's initial income. Alternatively he suggests that the proportion should rise from 6 — 16% of initial income up to a given income above which it would remain as a constant proportion. Thirdly, the allocation could be made on the basis of a proportionate rise throughout the range of income varying between 4–49% of initial income.[17] Cartter similarly provides three assumptions[18] and both authors arrive at similar conclusions concerning the most acceptable approximation — the almost completely progressive model of benefit allocation.

In terms of Barna's alternative, they both favour a solution between his second and third assumptions though nearer to the latter. Compared with these earlier methods of overcoming the difficulty of indivisible benefits, Nicholson's exclusion of them (which as he indicates had the same effect 'as would be obtained by allocating' them 'in proportion to each household's income')[19] is particularly unsatisfactory and productive of an element of spurious 'equality' within post-redistribution income figures.

Peacock and Shannon rightly note that by excluding indivisible benefits from their studies, Nicholson and the C.S.O. are working with government receipts which are double government expenditures. They suggest that the inevitable distortions are reflected in 'breakeven' incomes, which are too low. Allocating indivisible benefits would result in far more households paying zero or negative net taxation. A possible solution which they elaborate is to deduct only those taxes which can be assumed to be spent on the social services.[20]

Such a study of the redistribution effected through a narrowly defined system of social services would also be misleading. As we have just noted, indivisible benefits cannot be assumed to benefit everybody equally. For this reason we would advocate the preservation of the C.S.O. approach of allocating all taxes, but with the modification that indivisible benefits should be allocated preferably on two or more sets of assumptions. We feel that the resulting estimates would be more useful to policy discussions than those that would result from the kind of study suggested by Peacock and Shannon.

NOTES

1. Nicholson, J. L., op. cit., p. 9.
2. The evidence presented in Miss D. Nevitt's book (op. cit) of variations in local authority subsidies should be sufficient indication of the limitations of a national study which averages widely differing rates of local welfare provision.
3. We have already noted that children were over-sampled in the 1953–4 and 1960 Family Expenditure Surveys; this fact suggests that Nicholson's allocation of benefits may well be biased. See Abel-Smith, B., & Townsend, P. op. cit., p. 3.
4. Some of the factors affecting the payment of direct taxation are referred ¦to again in Chapter 6.
5. Nicholson, J. L., op. cit., p. 6.
6. Peacock and Shannon, op. cit., p. 42. They argue that once subjective considerations are included, only direct enquiry of each household as to their evaluation of benefits would resolve the problem of allocation.

7. There is some evidence of differential use by income groups of the high cost sectors of the National Health Service, for example, in Titmuss, R. M. and Abel-Smith, B., 'The Cost of the National Health Service in England and Wales', Cambridge University Press, 1956, Appendix H. This would suggest that the lower income groups may gain less from some of the more specialized health services. On the other hand Martin Rein has argued that the distribution of N.H.S. benefits favours low income groups— Rein, M., 'Health for Whom?', New Society, 20th November, 1969.

8. Recommendations on salary increases within the National Health Service provide an interesting example. The need would arise in a study using public expenditure figures with more reticence, to attempt to assess the proportion of the salary increases which represent an existing undervaluation of the benefits accruing to beneficiaries of the service, the proportion representing pending alterations in the quality of service provided and that proportion which may arise purely from the differential political power of the negotiating bodies. Nicholson, however, does not discuss the implications of his assumption that public expenditure may be utilized in quantifying the benefits provided by the social services.

9. Peacock and Shannon, op. cit., p. 40.

10. See 'Higher Education', Report of the Committee under the Chairmanship of Lord Robbins, Cmnd. 2154, London HMSO, 1963, Appendix 4, Part VI.

11. Ibid., Main Report, paragraphs 641–47 and Appendix II. Volume A, Part VI. In so far as the benefit generates income for the person in question it also alters his liability to taxation and his claims to and gain from benefits. Comparisons of longtitudinal redistribution patterns would provide data on which the apportioning of the cost of university education could take place, possibly suggesting the value of adjusting taxation, rather than the abolition of grants, in order to make the redistribution process more equitable.

12. The 'investment' value of a benefit refers to the possibility of lifetime incomes being enhanced by the receipt of that benefit. In short the term has been used to denote the possible effects of a benefit on the recipient's earning power. Benefits may also have investment value for a recipient in the sense of prolonging or enriching life itself, pensions fall within this category. In the sense we have attributed to the term, it underlines the impact that some benefits have on the future distribution of initial incomes.

13. The benefit from the increases were confined to lower income families by simultaneously modifying income tax allowances.

14. For a very useful discussion of negative income tax see Atkinson, A. B., 'Poverty in Britain and the Reform of Social Security', Cambridge University Press, Department of Applied Economics Occasional Papers 18, 1969 Chapter nine.

15. Indeed the attempt to treat groups of social welfare programmes as systems for analytical, planning and therefore administrative purposes, is an essential step in the development of social policy and administration.

16. Barna, T., op. cit. p. 208.

17. Ibid., p. 211. For the theoretical justification of these assumptions see pp. 208–11.

18. Cartter, A. M., op. cit., p. 50.

19. Nicholson, J. L., op. cit., p. 17.

20. Peacock and Shannon, op. cit., pp. 34–38.

6. THE VARIABLE TAX BURDEN BORNE BY FAMILIES

From the observations we made in the last two chapters on Nicholson's work it will be apparent that, if we exclude benefits as such, a true comparison of the relative burden of net taxation on families can only be made if:

(a) Additional income as we have defined it is included.[1] These forms of income are available to limited numbers of families only but may form a large part of their real incomes.

(b) Families rather than households are considered.

(c) Families where for example the wife is working, are treated separately from the other families in the same income and size range.

Separate calculations will therefore be made for different types of family in order to emphasize the differences in circumstances which exist *within* the income and family size ranges utilized by Nicholson. Our concern is to indicate the variations in the tax burden within income and family size groups and we have not attempted to allocate benefits generally.

The importance of owner occupation as a source of additional income is illustrated by our figures. As in Chapter 4 we have also included the subsidy accruing to local authority tenants. This subsidy is a welfare benefit and not additional income of the kind accruing to owner occupiers, but there is no comprehensive social service in housing and we have presented figures for both in order to provide a more complete picture of the importance of housing to the rate of net taxation paid. Nicholson's figures include estimates of the recorded subsidy accruing to local authority tenants, but not the concealed subsidy or the estimated additional income figures for owner occupiers that we include.

In accordance with our earlier comments on the allocation of taxation in the Nicholson/C.S.O. studies we are assuming that taxation borne by families consists of:—

Table 3—Expenditure Tax per Family Income and Size—1964

Income Range	(a) £ 559/ 676	(b) £ 676/ 816	(c) £ 816/ 988	(d) £ 988/ 1,196	(e) £ 1,196/ 1,448	(f) £ 1,448/ 1,752	(g) £ 1,752/ 2,122
Median	626	750	904	1,100	1,323	1,581	1,931
1 ADULT							
Expenditure tax	125.9	127.2	167.4	142.3	182.6	241.5	260·5
Employer's National Insurance contributions	16.3	19.2	22.3	26.9	33.0	37.9	48·0
TOTAL	142·2	146·4	189·7	169·2	215·6	279·4	308·5
COUPLE							
Expenditure tax	131·0	141·7	163·1	191·4	222·4	245·9	260·5
Employer's National Insurance contributions	19·4	21·8	24·5	28·5	34·0	40·1	48·0
TOTAL	150·4	163·5	187·6	219·9	256·4	286·0	308·5
COUPLE & 1 CHILD							
Expenditure tax	133·4	149·2	163·0	192·9	209·7	253·9	325·1
Employer's National Insurance contributions	19·1	21·0	24·4	29·6	34·8	40·3	46·7
TOTAL	152·5	170·2	187·4	222·5	244·5	294·2	371·8

COUPLE & 2 CHILDREN							
Expenditure tax	141·9	156·9	177·5	201·2	203·3	248·2	274·4
Employer's National Insurance contributions	18·6	21·3	25·8	30·4	35·8	42·0	49·4
TOTAL	160·5	178·2	203·3	231·6	239·1	290·2	323·8
COUPLE & 3 CHILDREN							
Expenditure tax		162·7	166·8	192·7	212·0	206·2	
Employer's National Insurance contributions		22·7	26·6	31·8	37·9	43·6	
TOTAL		185·4	193·3	224·5	249·9	249·8	

(1) It has been assumed that the ratio of expenditure tax per income range for families is the same as for households. This is correct for one adult families. There are no two adult households in the Family Expenditure Survey for 1964 which did not consist of one man and one woman only. Most of these are couples, married or otherwise, but some are not, e.g. father and adult daughter. Less than one per cent of households with two adults and one to three children included two men or two women. It is, therefore, likely that the divergence between families and households for the family sizes recorded here was small. A substantial proportion of households contain three or more adults (Table 7). It is in this category that the divergence between families and households mainly exists.

(2) Employer's National Insurance contributions enter into the cost of all home produced goods and services, including, indirectly, housing. The amount of contributions included in the price of the goods varies with the number and sex of the people employed and the ratio of expenditure tax to the cost of the articles or services. In the absence of more refined data, this tax has been calculated as a percentage of personal income less direct taxation and it has been assumed to be constant at 2.9%. The tax has been computed in the table by multiplying by this ratio income plus cash benefits less direct taxation, recorded in the C.S.O. study. It is realized that these estimates are subject to a wide margin of error.

81

TABLE 4—Net Tax Burden—One Earner—1964

Income p.a.	(a) £ 642	(b) £ 742	(c) £ 842	(d) £ 942	(e) £ 1,042	(f) £ 1,142	(g) £ 1,242	(h) £ 1,342	(i) £ 1,442	(j) £ 1,542
1 ADULT										
Employee's N.I.C.	33·5	33·5	33·5	33·5	33·5	33·5	33·5	33·5	33·5	33·5
Income Tax	73·1	101·3	131·6	161·8	192·0	221·8	252·0	282·2	312·5	342·6
Expenditure Tax	142·7	146·1	172·4	185·8	175·3	177·9	198·5	220·3	245·1	269·9
NET TAX—£	249·3	280·9	337·5	381·1	400·8	433·2	484·0	536·0	591·1	646·0
% of income	38·8	37·8	40·1	39·4	38·4	38·0	39·0	40·0	41·0	42·0
COUPLE										
Employee's N.I.C.	33·5	33·5	33·5	33·5	33·5	33·5	33·5	33·5	33·5	33·5
Income Tax	37·1	60·5	85·0	115·4	145·9	175·3	205·6	235·8	266·1	296·2
Expenditure Tax	152·1	162·7	178·0	193·9	210·2	226·8	242·9	258·6	270·0	281·5
NET TAX—£	222·7	256·7	296·5	342·8	389·6	435·6	482·0	527·9	569·6	611·2
% of income	34·7	34·6	35·2	36·4	37·4	38·2	38·8	39·4	39·5	39·7
COUPLE & 1 CHILD										
Employee's N.I.C.	33·5	33·5	33·5	33·5	33·5	33·5	33·5	33·5	33·5	33·5
Income Tax	3·4	19·0	41·9	65·3	91·6	121·1	151·3	191·4	211·6	241·6
Expenditure Tax	155·8	169·1	180·5	194·2	212·0	226·6	236·4	248·2	267·6	286·9
School Meals & Milk	(8·9)	(8·9)	(8·9)	(8·9)	(8·9)	(8·9)	(8·9)	(8·9)	(8·9)	(8·9)
NET TAX—£	183·8	212·7	247·0	284·1	328·2	372·3	412·3	464·2	503·8	553·1
% of income	28·6	28·7	29·4	30·2	31·5	32·6	33·2	34·6	34·9	35·9
COUPLE & 2 CHILDREN										
Employee/s N.I.C.	33·5	33·5	33·5	33·5	33·5	33·5	33·5	33·5	33·5	33·5
Income Tax	Nil	Nil	9·8	28·1	51·8	74·6	103·2	133·5	163·7	193·7
Expenditure Tax	162·8	177·1	193·3	208·8	223·1	233·0	236·3	242·8	262·6	282·6
Family All'ces & School Meals & Milk	(38·6)	(38·6)	(38·6)	(38·6)	(38·6)	(38·6)	(38·6)	(38·6)	(38·6)	(38·6)
NET TAX—£	157·7	172·0	198·0	231·8	269·8	302·5	334·4	371·2	421·2	471·2
% of income	24·6	23·2	23·8	24·6	25·9	26·5	27·0	27·7	29·3	30·6

COUPLE & 3 CHILDREN									
Employee/s N.I.C.	33·5	33·5	33·5	33·5	33·5	33·5	33·5	33·5	33·5	33·5
Income Tax	Nil	Nil	Nil	1·4	17·2	38·6	62·0	87·0	117·2	147·2
Expenditure Tax	180·2	184·8	190·2	199·4	215·1	229·3	240·5	249·9	249·9	249·8
Family All'ces & School Meals & Milk	(73·5)	(73·5)	(73·5)	(73·5)	(73·5)	(73·5)	(73·5)	(73·5)	(73·5)	(73·5)
NET TAX—£	140·2	144·8	150·2	160·8	192·3	227·9	262·5	296·9	327·1	357·0
% of income	21·8	19·5	17·8	17·1	18·5	20·0	21·1	22·1	22·7	23·2

(1) The middle band of child tax allowances has been used.
(2) Expenditure tax has been extrapolated from the figures in Table 3.

A comparison of our conclusions regarding the burden of net taxation as calculated by Nicholson with the figures in Table (4) differently computed reveals that:—

(i) In both cases expenditure taxation is regressive. Our figures show it to be more so than Nicholson's.

(ii) Nicholson found direct taxation—National Insurance contributions and income tax—to be only mildly progressive. Our table shows that it is more progressive.

(iii) According to Nicholson's calculations, net taxation is progressive in the lowest two income ranges and thereafter mildly so. Our figures show that in all income ranges and in all family sizes net taxation is only very slightly progressive. For one and two child families the net tax ratio of the highest income range was 25% greater than that of the lowest. For three child families the difference was negligible—only 6%. Here, net taxation was slightly regressive when family incomes were low.

(iv) The differences in the burden of net taxation on the different size family as shown in the table are smaller than in the Nicholson study. In average income range (d) the reduction in respect of a wife was 8% of the net taxation ratio, and the reduction for each child was about 18%. These ratios remain fairly constant throughout the income ranges. Counting a child as half a unit, we note that income per head of two child households was only 74% of that of households with two adults only. After net taxation the position is only slightly improved. The ratio of net income per head rises to only, 77% of that of a couple without children in the lowest income range. For average income groups (c) and (d) it rises to 79%. This ratio remains fairly constant and is the same in the highest income ranges. For three children families there is very little difference between income groups. Net income per head is about 73% to 75% of net income of families without children. Taxation therefore has very little impact upon the existing differentials in the per capita income received by different family types and these differentials remains fairly constant between income groups and family types.

(1) employees' National Insurance contributions;
(2) income tax;
(3) expenditure taxation. This includes domestic rates and taxes
    on intermediate products, e.g. industrial and commercial rates.
    It also includes employers' National Insurance contributions.
Data regarding indirect taxation are available in the C.S.O. studies
and these will be used, after adjustment, in our calculations. Expenditure taxation per family has been estimated on the basis of taxation
per household recorded in the C.S.O. study. The figures have been
grossed up to include employers' National Insurance contributions.
Estimated expenditure taxation per family is shown in Table (3).
From the sum of taxes, family allowances have been deducted.
These have been treated as a negative tax. The subsidy on school
meals and milk and welfare foods, amounting in 1964 to £8.9[2] per
child per annum, has been similarly treated.[3]

1. No additional income
(a) One Earner
In Table (4) the next tax burden has been calculated for a
number of family sizes and income ranges. The following assumptions have been made:—
  (i) That all income is earned.
  (ii) That there is only one income earner.
  (iii) That the average of contracted out and contracted in
        National Insurance contributions excluding graduated
        payments can reasonably be allocated to each family.
Average annual earnings of male manual workers, excluding those
in agriculture, in 1964 were £942 and net tax has been calculated for
this income range. Average income per couple and single person was
only slightly higher—£965. Similar calculations have been made for
income ranges £642 to £1,542. In 1964 16.4% of couples had incomes of under £600 per annum. Almost the same proportion of
couples had incomes over £1,500 per annum—16.6%.[4] Thus, our
range covers two-thirds of all married couples, excluding approximately the same proportion at the bottom as it does at the top. Only
for these income ranges are expenditure taxation data available in
respect of all family sizes in the C.S.O. study and the table has been
compiled accordingly.

Thus, using a different basis, our conclusions corroborate Nicholson's generally, but strongly emphasize the lack of progression. For
all families of a given size, net taxation represents almost a constant
proportion of income in all income ranges. The burden of net tax
borne by families with children at all income levels is only slightly
less than that of childless couples.

(b) *Wife Earning*

In 1964, 41% of wives had earned incomes. The proportion of better off families with working wives was higher than average. In the under £1,000 income range only 22% of wives had earnings, whereas when incomes exceeded £1,000 the ratio rose to 51%.[5] The increase in incomes is not entirely due to wives' earnings. It also results from the fact that a higher proportion of the wives of high income earners do work.

As is to be expected, more wives work when there are no children. The ratio of working wives with children to all working wives was 46%, whereas for the non-earners the proportion was 58% in 1964.[5]

This view is confirmed by the Ministry of Social Security's Report 'Circumstances of Family' (1967). Only 6% of families with children had weekly incomes of less than £3 above national assistance standards, when wives worked. The ratio when wives' earnings were not received was 15%.

In 1965[6] wives' earnings accounted for 14.5% of the joint earnings of husband and wife. As 41% of wives work, 35% of joint earnings must be contributed by working wives.

Total income tax is, of course, lower when incomes are split between two earner's, because the reduced rate reliefs are available on each earner's income. In addition, special tax relief of up to £120 is given to working wives. The personal allowances of two single people amounted to £400 in 1964 and that of a married couple was £320. Wife's earned income relief of up to £200 is available, increasing the total allowance to £520, £120 more than that granted to two single people.[7] In addition, the flat rate element of National Insurance contribution does not rise where wives' earnings increase family income.

Accordingly, the effect of wives' earnings is to make net taxation even more proportionate to income and to reduce the effective reliefs to large families, these effects are reflected in Table (5) and in Figure I.

(c) *Lack of Progression*

Factors contributing to the lack of progression of net taxation and the reduction in the differential enjoyed by large families are:—

> Employee's National Insurance contributions
> Child income tax allowances
> Domestic rates.

(i) *Employees' National Insurance Contributions*

The flat rate element of employees' National Insurance contributions is a poll tax and remains relatively constant whatever the earnings or

TABLE 5—Net Tax Burden—Wife Working—1964

Income p.a.	(a) £642	(b) £742	(c) £842	(d) £942	(e) £1,042	(f) £1,142	(g) £1,242	(h) £1,342	(i) £1,442	(j) £1,542
COUPLE										
NET TAX—£	193·6	216·4	248·2	286·8	325·5	366·6	410·6	456·9	498·3	541·8
% of income	30·2	27·9	29·5	30·4	31·2	32·1	33·0	34·0	34·5	35·2
COUPLE & 1 CHILD										
NET TAX—£	181·8	195·1	208·9	239·4	288·4	313·4	345·9	383·2	432·0	482·0
% of income	28·4	26·4	24·9	25·4	27·7	27·5	27·8	28·6	30·0	31·3
COUPLE & 2 CHILDREN										
NET TAX—£	159·1	173·4	189·6	210·7	230·4	258·5	278·9	298·3	355·6	400·5
% of income	24·8	23·4	22·5	22·4	22·1	22·7	22·5	22·3	24·7	26·9
COUPLE & 3 CHILDREN										
NET TAX—£	141·6	146·2	151·6	160·8	187·5	206·3	222·5	240·7	271·4	296·2
% of income	22·1	19·7	18·0	17·1	18·0	18·2	17·9	18·0	18·8	19·2

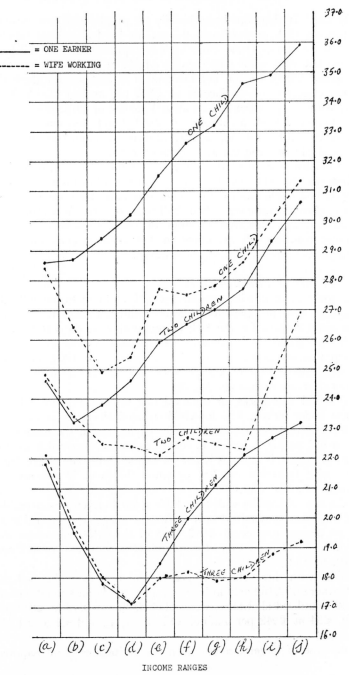

= ONE EARNER

= WIFE WORKING

ONE CHILD

ONE CHILD

TWO CHILDREN

TWO CHILDREN

THREE CHILDREN

THREE CHILDREN

PERCENTAGE OF INCOME

(a) (b) (c) (d) (e) (f) (g) (h) (i) (j)

INCOME RANGES

FIGURE 1—The net tax burden borne by families with only one earner and with a working wife (based on Tables 4 and 5)

family size.[8] It therefore bears heavily on people with low incomes and forms a high proportion of the net tax burden of large families with low incomes. These contributions represented only 5.2% of total net tax for a single man earning £1,542 in 1964. However, they represented 23.9% of the net taxation of a family with three dependent children and an income of £642 per annum (Table 5). A family with two children and an annual income of £642 paid £33 in direct taxation. With an income of £842 direct taxation remained £33. When income rises to, say £1,542 direct taxation consists of the same £33 plus income tax at progressive rates.

The burden is particularly heavy for families maintained by husbandless women. The average contribution per adult male was £33.5 in 1964. For single women the figure was only £6.5 less, although women's earnings were only about half those of men. As a proportion of male average industrial earnings in 1964, employees' National Insurance contributions amounted to 3.6%. For women the lower contributions represented 5.8% of earnings.

(ii) *Child Income Tax Allowances*

The inability of low income families with children to use fully the major state cash provision for children, child tax allowances, is one of the main reasons for the lack of progression in the net taxation paid by this group. As much as 78% of the cost of cash provision for children was accounted for by these allowances in 1964, and they were worth an average of £48 per annum to tax payers with annual incomes over approximately £1,300.

The actual allowances for standard rate tax payers were £45 for children under eleven, £54 for children aged eleven to sixteen and £64 for children over sixteen. Families paying tax at the margin (in 1964) at 6/– in the £ or 4/– in the £, of course, received a smaller benefit. If no tax is paid, as is not uncommon with very large families, or with fatherless families, or when the head is unemployed, no benefit at all is received.

In the case of families with two children aged eleven to sixteen, the full allowance was obtained only at income range (f) (See Table 5). With an annual income of £642, £66 of the £108 allowance was unused. At £842 per annum the unutilized portion fell to £27 and at £942 to £11.

Families with three children aged eleven to sixteen obtained the full allowance of £162 only in income range (h). At an annual income of £642 unutilized allowances were £114, falling to £73 at £842 per annum, £34 at £942 per annum, £12 at £1,142 and £4 at £1,242 per annum.

In the case of larger families, even higher incomes were required before the full allowance was obtainable. Families with three or more children have to have well above average incomes before the full allowance is received. This is especially the case where there are wives' earnings.

One of the virtues of the introduction of family allowances in 1946 was that these benefits were available to families largely deprived of the benefit of child income tax allowances. However the latter have risen by 45% since 1952 and the former had hardly risen at all by 1964.[9]

(iii) *Domestic Rates*

Rates constitute one of the more important expenditure taxes and contribute to the regression of this group. The average rate burden in 1963/64 was £30.6 in England and Wales and £32.7 in Scotland. Rate payment rose less than proportionately with income. In England and Wales households with under £312 per annum paid rates of £19.2, whereas households with over £1,560 paid only £42.9.[10] According to a survey carried out by the Allen Committee, rates represented 8.2% of household income after direct taxation for households with under £312 per annum and only 2.2% for those with over £1,560. The average for all income groups was 2.9%. This phenomenon was common to all regions.

Households with retired heads pay more in rates than earner households with the same income. This applies both to actual payments and to rates as a proportion of income after direct taxation. Thus, in the £520 to £1,040 income range retired heads in England and Wales paid £30.7 and earner heads only £24.4. This phenomenon occurred particularly with retired men or women living alone, except with incomes of under £312 per annum.

The size of the dwelling was found to be the most important single factor affecting rates. On average, each additional room added £6 per annum. Accordingly, families with a large number of children and occupying adequate accommodation could be expected to pay more in rates. In fact, their rate burden does not rise.[11] This may be partly due to the fact that many families in which the number of children increases cannot, or in the case of the better off do not need to move to, more spacious accommodation.

(2) *Additional Income*

In Table (6) the net tax burden as a proportion of revised income has been calculated for families occupying local authority dwellings and belonging to occupational pension schemes. In 1963/64 the mean income of local authority tenant households in England and Wales was £964—close to income range (d). For London the figure was

TABLE 6—Local Authority House Subsidy and Superannuation Contributions Net Tax Burden—1964

Original Income p.a.	(a) £642	(b) £742	(c) £842	(d) £942	(e) £1,042	(f) £1,142	(g) £1,242	(h) £1,342	(i) £1,442	(j) £1,542
Employer's Superann. Contributions	22	26	29	33	36	40	43	47	50	54
Revised Income	664	768	871	975	1,078	1,182	1,285	1,389	1,492	1,596
L/A House Subsidy	107	107	107	107	107	107	107	107	107	107
Employee's Superann. Contributions	15	18	20	23	25	27	30	32	34	37
1 ADULT										
NET TAX—£	138·8	168·5	224·5	267·1	286·3	318·1	367·9	419·3	473·9	517·9
NET TAX—% of Revised Income	20·9	21·9	25·8	27·4	26·6	27·0	28·7	30·2	31·8	32·4
COUPLE										
NET TAX—£	112·2	145·5	183·8	228·8	275·1	320·5	365·9	411·2	452·4	483·1
NET TAX—% of Revised Income	16·9	19·0	21·1	23·5	25·6	27·2	28·5	29·6	30·4	30·3
COUPLE & 1 CHILD										
NET TAX—£	74·5	102·9	135·4	170·7	213·7	257·2	296·2	347·5	386·6	425·0
NET TAX—% of Revised Income	11·6	13·8	16·1	18·1	20·5	21·8	23·1	25·0	26·0	26·6
COUPLE & 2 CHILDREN										
NET TAX—£	50·7	65·0	87·9	119·4	157·0	189·2	218·3	254·5	304·0	343·1
NET TAX—% of Revised Income	7·9	8·8	10·5	12·6	15·1	16·0	17·0	18·4	20·4	21·5
COUPLE & 3 CHILDREN										
NET TAX—£	33·2	37·8	43·2	52·4	81·4	113·6	148·5	180·6	209·9	228·9
NET TAX—% of Revised Income	5·2	5·1	5·1	5·6	7·8	9·6	11·6	13·0	14·1	14·3

Notes: This table has been computed from the figures in Table (4). It has therefore been assumed that there are no wives' earnings.
(1) Employer's superannuation and life assurance contribution has been calculated at 3½% of salary.
(2) Employee's contribution has been calculated at 3%. A reduction of 20% has been made from the tax saving.
(3) The average true local authority house subsidy, as estimated in Chapter V, has been used. As larger families occupy larger

£1,224. In the same year the mean income of other tenant households was £827 per annum in England and Wales and £982 in London.

The effect of these benefits is very great. A family with two children in income range (c) and no additional income bears almost double the ratio of net tax of a similar family in income range (d) living in a local authority dwelling and belonging to a superannuation scheme. For similar families with three children the ratio rises to over three. It drops for smaller families, but remains substantial in amount.

In Table (7) similar estimates have been made for owner-occupier families belonging to occupational pension schemes. The bottom three income ranges have been excluded, because few families with incomes of under £942 in 1964 lived in this type of accommodation. The median incomes of owner-occupier households in England and Wales and in London in 1963/64 were respectively £1,238 and £1,445.

It will be seen that the reduction in the burden of net taxation resulting from owner-occupation is less than from local authority tenancies. This is because the total estimated subsidy is only about equivalent to the undisclosed local authority figure and this is spread over many more dwellings.[12] For most owner-occupiers the subsidy amounts to about £48 per annum. On above-average priced houses the true subsidy rises and at £6,700 it is approximately the same as the local authority subsidy of £107 per annum.

In Table (8) the net tax burden of different sized families with average income are placed side by side. Where there is only one earned income the following conclusions emerge:—

(i) Owner-occupation and superannuation contributions reduce the net tax burden by about 15% for all family sizes.

(ii) Local authority tenancies and superannuation contributions reduce the net tax burden by an average of about 42%. The proportionate reduction rises with the size of the family.

Where part of the income is contributed by a wife, the proportionate net tax burden falls further. Comparing a family with a working wife, living in a local authority dwelling and belonging to an occupational pension scheme on the one hand, with a one earner family with no additional income on the other, the net tax burden of the former is only 40% of the latter if there are one or two children. For childless couples it is about half. For larger families the full net taxation benefits are only obtainable at higher incomes.

The next tax burden of a childless couple in a local authority dwelling with an original income of £1,242 per annum is lower than that of a family with two children, no additional income and annual earnings of £642.

TABLE 7—Income Including Imputed Owner-Occupier Rent and Superannuation Contributions—1964

Original Income per annum	(d) £942	(e) £1,042	(f) £1,142	(g) £1,242	(h) £1,342	(i) £1,442	(j) £1,542
Imputed Rent	126	136	146	156	156	156	156
Employer's Superannuation Contributions	33	36	40	43	47	50	54
Revised Income	1,101	1,214	1,328	1,441	1,545	1,648	1,752
Employee's Superannuation Contributions	23	25	27	30	32	34	37
1 ADULT							
NET TAX—£	374·1	393·3	425·1	474·9	526·3	580·9	624·9
% of Revised income	34·0	32·4	32·1	33·0	34·1	35·3	35·7
COUPLE							
NET TAX—£	335·8	382·1	427·5	472·9	518·2	559·4	590·1
% of Revised Income	30·7	31·5	32·2	32·9	33·6	34·0	33·7
COUPLE & 1 CHILD							
NET TAX—£	277·7	320·7	364·2	403·2	454·5	493·6	532·0
% of Revised Income	25·2	26·4	27·4	28·0	29·4	30·9	30·4
COUPLE & 2 CHILDREN							
NET TAX—£	226·4	264·0	296·2	325·3	361·5	411·0	450·1
% of Revised Income	20·6	21·8	22·3	22·6	23·4	25·0	25·7
COUPLE & 3 CHILDREN							
NET TAX—£	159·4	188·4	221·6	255·5	287·6	316·9	335·9
% of Revised Income	14·5	15·5	16·7	17·7	18·6	19·2	19·2

Notes: (1) The superannuation contribution figures have been taken from Table (6).
(2) The average notional rent of £156 has been used for the top four income ranges. Lower rents have been used for families with below average owner-occupier incomes.

TABLE 8
Net Tax Burden—1964—Original Income £942

| | No Additional Income | | Additional Income | | | |
| | | | Imputed Rent and Superannuation Contributions | | Local Authority Subsidy and Superannuations Contributions | |
	1 Earner	Wife Working	1 Earner	Wife Working	1 Earner	Wife Working
1 ADULT						
NET TAX—£	381.1	—	374·1	—	267·1	—
—% of Revised Income	39.4	—	34·0	—	27·4	—
COUPLE						
NET TAX—£	342.8	286·8	335·8	279·8	228·8	172·8
—% of Revised Income	36·4	30·4	30·7	25·4	23·5	17·7
COUPLE & 1 CHILD						
NET TAX—£	284·1	239·4	277·7	233·0	170·7	126·0
—% of Revised Income	30·2	25·4	25·2	21·2	18·1	12·9
COUPLE & 2 CHILDREN						
NET TAX—£	231.8	210·7	226·4	205·3	119·4	98·3
—% of Revised Income	24·6	22·4	20·6	18·6	12·6	10·1
COUPLE & 3 CHILDREN						
NET TAX—£	160·8	160·8	159·4	159·4	52·4	52·4
—% of Revised Income	17·1	17·1	14·5	14·5	5·6	5·6

Note: This table has been compiled from the figures in Tables (4), (5), (6) and (7).
in income range (d).

(3) *Higher Incomes*

On higher incomes, up to over £4,000 per annum, the effective marginal rate of income tax is constant at 30%. Such incomes represent only a small proportion of the total. In 1964 incomes of over £3,000 per annum accounted for only 2% of all incomes.[13]

Assuming that the rise in expenditure taxation is proportionate to the increase between the lowest and highest income ranges in Table (8), at £3,000 the net tax ratio would be:—

Couple	42.0%
Couple and 1 child	40.0%
Couple and 2 children	36.8%

If this assumption is correct there is hardly any change in the ratio of net tax for families without children when incomes are doubled to

£3,000. With the addition of children the ratio rises, but only moderately. A family on £642 with two children paid 26% of their income in net taxation in 1964, whereas one with £3,000 per annum paid only 1½ times this ratio.

In their 'Poor and the Poorest' Abel-Smith and Townsend took as the limit of poverty 140% of the national assistance basic scale plus rent and rates. A family with two children on £642 per annum in 1964 were living at this defined limit of poverty and yet were required to pay a quarter of their income in tax.

It is probable that the degree of progression of net taxation is small even when incomes of up to £4,000 are included.

Conclusions –

At the beginning of chapter three we summarized Nicholson's findings, that net taxation is progressive for the lowest income households and thereafter proportionate and that households with children bear substantially less net taxation at all income levels, than do childless households. From our own estimates it is apparent that the burden of net taxation, measured as a ratio of net income, is only very slightly progressive and the differences in the tax borne by larger and smaller families are not great.

The most important point which we wish to emphasize, however, is that these findings represent the averaged experiences of households which are differentiated only on the basis of their initial income and their composition. If one isolates, as we have, the effect of working wives on the incidence of net taxation the situation changes considerable. The taxation borne by families is reduced if the wife is working, the incidence of net taxation is even more proportionate (less progressive) in such families than in all households and the relative advantage enjoyed by larger families is reduced. Similarly, if families receiving additional income are isolated it can be seen that they pay a reduced ratio of their real incomes in net taxation.

Accordingly, the true burden of net taxation depends heavily on factors other than the family income; factors which are generally ignored by students of the subject.[14] The ratio of net tax payable has become haphazard. It depends on whether one is lucky enough to get a council house; whether one's income is high enough to get a mortgage; or one's job provides a pension. It also depends on whether the children can be left during the day or whether work is available near her home to enable the mother to work at advantageous tax rates.

The Nicholson/C.S.O. studies provide much valuable information on the processes of income redistribution, but they have not been designed to reveal the variability in the incidence of taxation that we have underlined in this chapter. In the absence of more research data on these nuances of the taxation system (and of the social welfare systems), the findings of income redistribution studies can prove misleading. The Nicholson/C.S.O. studies can be usefully supplemented by the kind of estimates we have made in this chapter and the conclusion we wish to emphasize is that the existing studies do not constitute a very adequate basis from which to discuss or evaluate the operation of social policies.

In our final chapter we elaborate on this point and finally summarize the findings which the C.S.O. studies have produced.

NOTES

1. Those items of 'additional' income that particularly concern us were discussed in Chapter 4.

2. Calculated after deducting from the total cost contributions not paid by parents of poor children and milk for expectant mothers.

3. Net taxation therefore amounts in our estimates to total taxation minus a few specified social welfare benefits. These are the subsidies to local authority housing, schools meals, milk and welfare foods and also family allowances. The inclusion of other benefits would entail a wide number of assumptions about the allocation of these benefits. We have excluded them so as not to obscure our main interest, the variability in the rate of taxation paid by families *within* the Nicholson/C.S.O. classification by income and family size.

4. 109th Report—Commissioners of Inand Revenue. Missing incomes apply more to single people than to married couples.

5. 109th Report of the Commissioners of Inland Revenue.

6. Family Expenditure Survey, 1965.

7. The Royal Commission on Taxation, 1954, recommended a reduction in the relief on wives' earnings but this recommendation has never been implemented. High joint earned incomes, although benefiting from this relief, are jeopardized by aggregation for earned income relief and surtax purposes. Thus, if husband and wife have joint earned incomes of over about £4,500, total tax is considerably higher than if they were single.

8. Different rates of contribution are paid by juveniles and adults and by men and women. The total contributions paid by a family therefore vary, but not consistently with need or family income.

9. The increased family allowances which commenced in April 1968, more than restored the purchasing power of the original allowances fixed in 1946. However, they do represent a lower proportion of earnings than the 1946 allowances.

10. Allen Report, op. cit.

11. Economic Trends No. 154, August 1966.

12. We have estimated the total additional income accruing to all owner occupiers in the form of notional rent. The subsidy to the owner occupier arises because tax is not paid on this notional income. Individual owner occupiers may obviously receive a larger subsidy through this form of tax relief than the average council tenant receives, our figures are averages. We have given no indication of the value of exemption from capital gains tax to the owner occupier in the above comparison.

13. 109th Report of the Commissioners of Inland Revenue.

14. Lydall H. F., in 'British Income and Savings' does make an allowance for retirement provision.

(1) *Methodological Problems*

A large number of critical comments of existing redistribution studies have been made in the preceding chapters and these need to be related to the categorization of methodologies set out in chapter two. Our critical remarks fall into two groups. Firstly, we have suggested that the formation and evaluation of social policy requires data from a number of different kinds of studies using different assumptions and techniques, whereas the Nicholson/C.S.O. studies employ an essentially unchanging set of techniques and definitions and can supply only a limited amount of the needed data. Secondly, within the methodology chosen, these researchers have been faced with many problems, not all of which have been overcome.

These latter difficulties may be briefly summarized. We have concentrated our attention on a few major problem areas; the inadequacy of incomes data and the absence of information on non-monetary and other 'additional' income; the uncertainties involved in allocating benefits, especially benefits in kind; the deficiencies of the Family Expenditure Survey, especially its poor coverage of minority groups (i.e. high income groups and large families); and finally the neglect, which is inevitable in a single national study of this type, of some relevant variables (the importance of working wives is one such variable that we drew attention to in the last chapter).

Our other group of criticisms emphasizes the need for studies additional to those conducted by the C.S.O. to throw light on some of the problems that the C.S.O. studies are not designed to consider. One of the most important in this category is the isolation of the redistributive potential of all forms of benefits (fiscal, occupational and social) which give recognition to social needs (i.e. studies falling within our category two in chapter two). There are also the complicating effects of the cumulative impact of some benefits and the fact that much redistribution takes place through time and not necessarily between income groups; these phenomena cannot be studied within the context of the Nicholson/C.S.O. research. It is for this reason that we outlined in chapter two the kinds of research programmes that would be necessary to provide really satisfactory data.

The conclusion which we have been suggesting is that, while substantial improvements have arisen from Nicholson's endeavours, these studies do not provide an exhaustive coverage of the field in which we are interested and even within the present limits of coverage they could be improved upon. We must, therefore, explicitly indicate such progress as could be reasonably hoped for in the not too distant future.

The first and perhaps the most important lies with the student of social administration and not the statistician. It has been emphasized that little is known of the patterns of actual receipt of social benefits. Somewhat belatedly perhaps, the magnitude of this particular lacuna is being recognized and a growing amount of interest is being shown in the factors which correlate with and explain this phenomena. Successful attempts to reduce non-utilization of appropriate service will certainly reduce the distortions produced in the allocation of welfare benefits to income groups. The creation of the Supplementary Benefits Commission and its success in attracting new clients is a notable example of this trend.[1] However, the findings of Davies and Reddin on the utilization of school meals are more important to income redistribution studies.[2] Both emphasize the importance of regional and local variations and thereby confirm the degree to which information is sacrificed and distortions are introduced when benefits are allocated to income groups in a national study.

Local and regional studies of redistribution would represent a considerable advance in that they would indicate the redistributive effectiveness of local social policies, and also the extent to which regional differences in the distribution of social and industrial capital are compounded or offset by the operation of welfare programmes. The continuing interest in regional development policies and the beginnings of positive discrimination based on smaller geographical areas make such avenues of progress especially pertinent. Some developments in social service administration can clearly reduce the under-utilization of services and bring patterns of actual usage nearer to those assumed in the computation of income redistribution. Conversely, however, some administrative developments are producing an increasingly complex and locally variable distribution of services, and a national study of redistribution cannot possibly reflect these.

One of the most important expectations for the future is, therefore, the development of local and regional studies of income distribution, social service utilization and income redistribution. This suggestion is

G

in accord with political and administrative trends at present, and it may even be hoped that the future units of local government could sponsor such studies independently or in consortium. The cost of the research needed is a powerful inhibiting factor and studies of the distribution of need are likely to prove more attractive in all but the most deprived regions. In the latter, data on incomes and social service utilization could prove to be directly relevant in the competition for nationally allocated resources. In view of these various factors it is to be hoped that some local and regional studies may be initiated at a national level (by the C.S.O.) in the near future.

Linked with the interest in welfare service utilization is the much neglected need to conduct research into 'subjective' benefits (the responses and expectations of the clients of these services). It was argued in chapter five that subjective criteria should not be utilized in allocating benefits and the absence of information was not the only reason for our making this assertion. Even a dramatic expansion of data in this area would not warrant changing the entire basis of benefit allocation in Nicholson's studies, for example. In so far as objective inequalities continue to underlie arguments for welfare policies that have redistributive features, there remains a need for correspondingly objective measures of patterns of inequality. It is also difficult to foresee any meaningful study based on subjective criteria being a technical possibility. However, the limited uses to which data on subjective factors can be put, must not lead us to underestimate their importance. It is not merely the difficulty of placing redistribution statistics into their human context which is important, but also our profound ignorance of the dimensions of this context. Consequently any research with a 'client orientation' must be seen as a helpful means of outlining the limitations of our statistical information. In services where 'utilization' by the appropriate groups of persons is virtually complete (i.e. education between the statutory age limits), the subjective factors become particularly prominent and a plea for further utilization studies is very much a plea for study of the client's response to the service and the benefits which it offers.

A further development that may be hoped for is that of 'individualizing' to some extent the findings which the Nicholson/C.S.O. studies have produced. In evaluating the effect of systems of social welfare, the redistribution of income between broad income groups is a first and necessary task. The existing studies have been developed to fulfil this need. Two complimentary types of study could provide information in addition to the global estimates of redistribution already available. One is the analysis of net taxation borne by particular groups of the population and following from this the study of individual families. In the first, attention could be usefully concentrated upon such groups as the retired population. In this instance a comparison of benefits received from all sources and of the publicly financed redistributive elements in these benefits, could be made between groups of the retired classified by reference to pre-retirement income. The patterns of inequality and redistribution pre and post-retirement is of considerable interest, but existing studies are not designed to shed light on this problem.

Classifying the population by type of accommodation could also prove a valuable way of concentrating on groups of beneficiaries which are not currently identified. Other examples are not difficult to suggest, the patterns of redistribution benefiting large families from different income groups, or the disabled, and a number of other such topics warrant close study. Indeed traditional studies of need with respect to most contingencies could usefully be augmented by consideration of the redistributive consequences of existing and proposed provisions. In all these examples the major need is to gather adequate basic data. The Family Expenditure Surveys have not really been large enough to permit closer analysis than that already undertaken. If the higher income groups or larger households were subdivided by housing characteristics the numbers involved would become hopelessly inadequate. Moreover, in the case of larger groups, such as the elderly, the additional data that would permit new methods of analysis (information on pre-retirement incomes) is difficult to obtain without incurring high survey costs. Conversely, it is because information is now available on the redistributive patterns in the population as a whole that the experiences of smaller groupings are important. Consequently, some progress may be attainable through smaller research studies.

The further degree of individualization involved in studying the impact of redistribution on particular families involves similar merits and problems. A national sample of the population could not possibly be classified by sufficient variables to isolate the situation of individual families. The position of families where the wife is an income earner was illustrated in the previous chapter. But 'model families' can be constructed from assumptions about family composition, income and social service utilization and the impact of changes in social policy can be measured against such models. The point of such an exercise is that the types of family assumed to be critically affected by given changes, or statistically average families, can be constructed in model form and relatively rapid calculations can be made of the marginal incidence of policy developments. The problems of estimating taxation and social service utilization are not removed by this procedure, however. In the previous chapter we utilized data from the Nicholson/C.S.O. study to construct a few types of family and these we generalized across income ranges. We were dependent therefore upon data from Nicholson's work to construct our estimates.

The Cases For and Against Abolishing the C.S.O. Studies

The possibility of using such a technique to concentrate on particular problems introduces a point of more general significance, which has been raised by Peacock and Shannon.[3] They rightly argue that, given the manifest difficulties of allocating taxes and benefits in theory as well as in practice, the measurement of marginal changes as opposed to absolute levels of redistribution is open to far fewer criticisms. The approximate impact on income redistribution of different types of policy proposal is the kind of information required by the decision-maker and the present studies are not designed to produce such information. Indeed the effect of new and experimental policies cannot be monitored at all rapidly at present. There is ample room for the development of flexible measures of the marginal effects of policy change and the findings of such studies would be a useful addition to the policy formation process.

Peacock and Shannon do not advocate additional studies of marginal changes. Their stance is that the Nicholson/C.S.O. studies are too unsatisfactory, at a theoretical level, to be worth continuing. They concentrate their attention upon a number of theoretical difficulties that Nicholson and the C.S.O. have not resolved, some of which we have not considered as yet.

One of their major criticisms concerns the partial allocation of benefits, which we have considered at some length. They particularly stress the distortions introduced by not allocating 'indivisible benefits' (defence and environmental services expenditure, for example). One of their recommended solutions is to construct a 'synthetic welfare budget' to consider only the redistribution affected by social welfare benefits and those elements of the taxation system which may be considered to finance these benefits.[4] They do not examine, as we have, the fact that such a budget represents the redistributive effects of only one sector of the social welfare system. The value of taxation based benefits are at least represented in full in Nicholson's calculations of tax burdens. In the Peacock/Shannon social welfare budget it would be far more difficult to reflect the role of these benefits. This problem could be solved most readily by allocating presently unallocated benefits on a number of different assumptions, as was suggested in chapter four. Peacock and Shannon stress that the exclusion of indivisible benefits affects the calculation of 'break even' points (the point at which family incomes and size result in the payment of zero net tax). By allocating indivisible benefits one would push the break-even point for each family type to a higher income level.

This is an undoubted weakness of the present studies, but our criticism is somewhat different. We have stressed that in calculating Gini coefficients of inequality the non-allocation of benefits is the same as allocating them in proportion to household income. We would, therefore, agree with them that the official studies should include alternative sets of calculations based upon different assumptions about the correct distribution of indivisible benefits.[5] To concentrate upon a social welfare budget (which is the alternative suggestion made by Peacock and Shannon) does not seem a satisfactory procedure. The only sense in which we would support such a narrowing of the field of study is in tracing the distribution of social recognition accorded to social needs whether this recognition takes the form of fiscal, occupational or social welfare benefits. This kind of study has been presented in this paper as a supplement to existing research and we do not see any such narrowly based study as an acceptable *alternative* to the official research programme.

Having stated our own view let us note the reasons Peacock and Shannon develop for preferring the marginal approach (the study of change) and for rejecting the Nicholson approach, at least in its present form. Estimating the redistributive effect of governmental policy in the provision of benefits (and the raising of taxes for these purposes) implies a comparison with a base line which is not specified. As they rightly note this base line is a hypothetical situation in which such governmental policies do not exist. The transition from the actual to the hypothetical situation does not involve the simple removal of redistributive services and taxes. At the very least the existence of these services implies a modification of employment patterns compared with the hypothetical non-redistributive society. The comparison that is implied in Nicholson's type of study is, therefore, a misleading one, for the hypothetical base line is not simply related to the society which is being studied. This is the most powerful argument deployed by Peacock and Shannon. All the detailed methodological problems which they and we have considered are insignificant alongside this fundamental theoretical objection. They rest their case for confining interest to marginal developments in policy on this argument.

Our position is different; we have assumed the necessity of some substantial degree of state social welfare provision. Our intention has been to consider the value of present data on redistribution in evaluating changes in this welfare system. In the main we have concentrated on the ability of the data to provide evaluation of past changes in social policy and in the last few pages we have noted the need for evaluation of proposed future changes. In the next section we discuss the question of how far social policy results in income redistribution in any one year, and the argument advanced by Peacock and Shannon must be present as an essential caveat in that discussion. Our major concern, however, is to ask how far income redistribution and income inequality has changed *over time as a result of changes in social policy*. In this context we stressed, at an early stage in this paper, that the Nicholson/C.S.O. studies are most valuable precisely because they permit some comparisons to be made over time.

There can be no entirely satisfactory answer to the key theoretical problem raised by Peacock and Shannon; redistribution studies do not and cannot compare the distribution of post-redistribution income in our present society with that which would obtain if the social services did not exist. Income redistribution studies provide evidence about the redistribution which is produced by providing benefits and raising finances through taxation for this purpose. This they do imperfectly and with much effort, estimation and compromise over methodology. What they cannot begin to do is to estimate the redistribution of initial incomes which occurs when a society establishes social services, modifies a market-based equilibrium and modifies the role, power and rates of growth of various service occupations.

Nevertheless, Nicholson's study of total income redistribution and of income inequality is of fundamental importance to social policy. Without such studies the marginal impact of policy changes (where these can be calculated) can only be related to *assumptions* about the existing level of income redistribution and inequality. For this reason we cannot agree with Peacock and Shannon that 'it is difficult to justify (the) continuance, at least in their present form' of the official studies.[6] We diverge from them both in stressing the problems of welfare benefit allocation more strongly than tax allocation problems and also in suporting the continuance of the official research studies even in their present form. Both of these divergences arise primarily from our intention of only considering the value of the official studies to the discussion of social policy making.

We also concur with them on several points. The official research data need to be hedged around with more qualificatory explanations. The research design does not include the role of the capital account in generating and maintaining inequality. This limitation is made clear in that the findings relate only to income; but the implications need to be spelled out in some detail. As we have noted, social services themselves have 'investment effects' and treating them merely as consumption services is as unsatisfactory as is excluding capital as a source of income and as a taxed commodity.

102

We equally agree that the present studies would be more useful if they included sets of findings based on different assumptions. We have particularly emphasized the value from our point of view of additional data in which 'notional taxes' are deducted and tax allowances are allocated as benefits. These important modifications could be made more or less immediately. More rigorous accounts of non-monetary income and the actual utilization of welfare services are desirable, but they cannot be produced by the C.S.O. The first would depend upon the sampling of data compulsorily collected by the Board of Inland Revenue and it would involve the modification of current income and tax-unit definitions. Such a prospect is not very likely and even if it were possible it would not yield entirely accurate results. Improvements of the latter kind depend upon students of social administration and very much need to be developed for the benefit of our subject as a whole.

In the ideal world, the income distribution data that we should like to see available would arise from studies conducted along each of the lines suggested in chapter two, including a large scale longitudinal study to eliminate the effects of redistribution over one person's lifetime and the problem of families of similar income level occupying different points in their respective life-income cycles. In the short term we have indicated a range of possible future methodological modifications and a substantial number of reasons for approaching the findings of all income distribution studies with caution. We now turn to a resumé of the findings of the Nicholson/C.S.O. studies.

(2) *THE RESULTS: HOW REDISTRIBUTIVE IS THE WELFARE STATE?*

(i) *The redistribution effected in any one year*

At the beginning of this book we made the assertion that the social services are redistributive. One of the most valuable aspects of Nicholson's work is that it indicates the enormous complexity of the redistributive processes and this despite our cautionary remarks about the simplification of these processes which is necessary when they are represented statistically.

Nevertheless, some generalizations are possible and we shall attempt to present these simply, while also indicating some of the complexity of our subject. If one considers the redistributive processes operating in any one year Nicholson's findings indicate that a significant degree of positive vertical redistribution takes place. This is most effectively revealed by the Gini coefficients of inequality calculated from the data gathered in 1953, 1957 and 1959. The Gini coefficient is a measure of the deviation from absolute equality (where all income units receive equal incomes) of the actual distribution of incomes in question.[7] The larger the coefficient the greater is the degree of inequality.

In 1959 the coefficient for pre-redistribution incomes was 32.1 and that for post-redistribution incomes was 25.1. Vertical redistribution, therefore, effected a reduction of inequality of seven points or marginally under 22%. In 1957 the impact of the redistributive process had been very similar, producing a reduction of inequality of 20.5%.[8]

The effect of the total redistribution process in 1953 cannot be represented in the same way, but the reduction in inequality produced by direct benefits and taxes alone was approximately 25%. The effect of direct benefits and taxes only was almost identical in 1959.[9] Total redistribution is less marked than that resulting from direct taxes and benefits due to the regressive nature of indirect taxes.

These figures indicate that a surprisingly constant and clearly significant degree of vertical redistribution per annum was taking place during at least three years of the fifties. These findings are obviously subject to all the qualifications that we have discussed. In particular the criticisms forwarded by Peacock and Shannon, which we discussed in the last section, are valid. The measure of redistribution effected in a single year does not reflect all the changes in income distribution which result from the existence of social and other public services. Despite all the uncertainties, we may still conclude with some confidence that the net effect of allocating taxes and benefits on Nicholson's assumptions is the reduction of income inequality by a worthwhile amount in each of these years. Our comments on the method of allocating benefits lead us to believe that the amount of redistribution has been overestimated by Nicholson.

Gini coefficients have not been published for the years since 1959 and a simple overall measure of the redistribution occurring during the sixties is, therefore, not available. The pattern of redistribution during these later years is most immediately observable in the tables presenting post-redistribution income as a proportion of pre-redistribution income and, as Nicholson notes, there are only minor changes in this general pattern over the whole period of the sixties.[10]

The types of family, by family size and income, which received more in all benefits than they paid in taxes, remained fairly constant during the years 1959-69. Typically families consisting of one adult paid more in taxes than they received in benefits in each of these years if they had an initial income of more than approximately £300.[11] A family of two adults and two children could have received on average an income of between £550 and £670 per annum without reaching the point at which they paid more in taxes than they received. A family with three children could have received up to approximately £1,200 before reaching this 'break even' point. The 'break even' incomes rose slowly but steadily during this period and this movement helped offset the effects of changes in living costs. These points can only be estimated with any degree of certainty for a very few family types and the data are only available as a general indication of the types of family who benefit most from the incidence of benefits and taxation. However, they can also be of some value in indicating possible trends of interest. It is worth noting, for example, that the 'break even' points for families containing one and two children were rising more quickly than for families with three children, during the mid-sixties.[12] The less favourable position of the slightly larger families is obviously of importance if the statistical trend accurately portrays changes in the incidence of net taxation.

Above the income level of £1,200, families of all types for which figures are published (families with up to four children) paid significantly more in taxation than they received in welfare benefits. Thus, families with two children, receiving £1,750 to £2,100 per annum retained approximately 85% of their income. Families of two adults and no children with similar incomes would have retained about 70% of their initial income.

All taxes net of all (allocated) benefits are, therefore, vertically progressive and to a limited extent they also appear to be horizontally progressive throughout the period 1953 to 1969 covered by the Nicholson/C.S.O. data. However, the progressiveness falls away sharply after the 'break even' points are reached, for each family type, and thereafter a fairly constant proportion of initial income is retained by higher income families. Our own estimates (see Chapter 6) suggest that the vertical incidence of taxation is basically proportionate and less progressive than that of taxation net of all benefits. We have also stressed the role of other variables (such as working wives) in reducing the progressiveness of taxation and making the analysis of income distribution a very complex procedure.

The sensitivity of taxes and benefits in effecting horizontal as opposed to vertical redistribution is difficult to assess. While it is clear that taxes net of benefits bear less heavily on families as family size increases, this is not dramatically so and its significance is difficult to judge. Family size is itself correlated with income and this is a relationship whch may be of importance even within income groups when fairly broad income categories are being used. Furthermore the weight which ought to be attached to each increase in a family's size and, therefore, in the family's needs) is not known. Consequently a given bias in favour of larger families cannot be said to be adequate or otherwise.[13]

A measure of inequality which took account of the changing income needed to maintain a constant standard of living as family size changed, might produce different estimates of the amount of redistribution effected in our society. Nicholson notes that using such a vertical-cum-horizontal measure, all taxes and benefits combined produced a greater reduction in inequality than is reflected in the published vertical redistribution figures.[14] This is the only, very slender, indication available of the likely effects on estimated levels of inequality of using this kind of measure.

Thus far we have given a general indication of the extent of overall redistribution achieved in the years from the early fifties to the late sixties. In the table below we have isolated the effects of the main groups of taxes and benefits. There have been few changes in the general incidence of these taxes and benefits and it is therefore not too misleading to present such a summary table. However, it must be emphasized that these remarks reflect the structure of taxation and welfare provision during the years in question. Changes in taxation or welfare policy could substantially modify this picture by altering the incidence of taxes or benefits.

Several further considerations may be added to this summary. Over the whole period the proportion of incomes taken in taxation and received in benefits has been rising slowly. The position with regard to benefits may be illustrated by considering the families which gained most from them. Households of two persons in the lowest income group received benefits equal to 53% of their income (defined for this purpose as original income plus cash benefits) in 1961; this figure had risen to 75% in 1967. Similarly households of two adults and two children received benefits equal to 28% of income (as defined above) in 1961 and 56% of income in 1967.[15] But these figures are for the groups receiving most benefit and average net taxation (after the receipt of all benefits) for all family types and income groups, looks rather different. In the years 1961 to 1963 an average of 13% of income was paid out in net taxation and by 1967 this had risen to 17%.[16] On average therefore, while benefits and taxes were both increasing as a proportion of income during the sixties, it was the value of benefits that increased more slowly.

Indirect Taxes

The incidence of indirect taxation, summarized in the table, is measured in the Nicholson studies against an approximation to disposable income. Disposable income in this context is the income available after the deduction of direct taxes and the allocation of bene-

DIRECT BENEFITS Vertical	Very Progressive (But some of these benefits are the most difficult items to allocate and may be most subject to error)	The July 1968[1] (Low Income Households) results indicate that for pensioner households, retirement and other pensions, followed by National Assistance payments dominate the pattern of benefit receipt. For low income families with children, education, followed by the NHS is the dominant source of benefits, family allowances are the most important cash benefits. Due to the difficulty of allocating NHS and education benefits, the redistribution favouring low income families with children may well be overestimated.
Horizontal	Favour large families more than any other group of benefits or taxation.	

INDIRECT BENEFITS Vertical	Progressive. They are progressive to a large extent because they are concentrated on lower income groups (council house tenants) but their incidence *within* lower income categories may not be progressive in particular local authority areas.
Horizontal	Favour large families but not to a very noticeable degree. (This tendency may be underestimated in earlier years.)

DIRECT TAXATION		Very progressive at the top and bottom of the income scale; much less so in the middle income ranges.
Vertical	INCOME and SURTAX	
	NATIONAL INSURANCE CONTRIBUTIONS	Regressive Graduated contributions are much less regressive than flat rate contributions.
Horizontal	INCOME and SURTAX	Favours large families at 'medium' incomes, at higher incomes the progression is much less relevant to larger families.
	NATIONAL INSURANCE CONTRIBUTIONS	Regressive Amount paid depends on number of employed persons in household and not on the number of dependents.

INDIRECT TAXATION Vertical	Regressive. The *amounts* paid are larger at higher income levels, but are a smaller *proportion* of these incomes.	The July 1968 results indicate that approximately the same proportion of disposable income is taken in all low, even in the very lowest, income groups; the taxes are therefore referred to as 'neutral' in incidence. As a proportion of original rather than disposable income the taxes would be definitely regressive.
Horizontal	Regressive. There is little variation by family size and they therefore favour smaller families.	

ALL TAXATION	Direct and indirect taxes combined constitute a remarkably constant proportion of the incomes of each of the main types of family over a wide range of incomes. The July 1968 results emphasize that this is so with the exception only of the very lowest income ranges and only small variations occur by family size.

(1) Economic Trends, July 1968.

fits. While this is an acceptable basis for measuring the effects of taxes on expenditure, indirect taxes would appear far more regressive than at present if they were presented as percentages of original income. The progressive effects of benefits and direct taxes are partly masking the regressive incidence of indirect taxes. The regressiveness of policy changes which reduce the progression obtained through direct benefits and taxes, or which substantially increased indirect taxation, is not fully reflected in the Nicholson/C.S.O. data. Equally if Nicholson's work over-estimates the degree of progression currently achieved through benefits and direct taxation then his data are already under-presenting the importance of indirect taxes as a regressive instrument of economic and fiscal policy.

This summary of the incidence of different types of taxation and benefits clearly underlines several obvious policy conclusions. Greater redistribution can be most easily effected by increasing direct benefits, all other factors remaining constant. These benefits produce greater equality by 'levelling up' and they do so with the maximum advantage accruing to larger families that it is possible to attain within our present fiscal and welfare systems. This horizontal progression largely results from the benefits in kind rather than those in cash. Nevertheless, this conclusion is less simple than it seems for we have noted that the allocation of benefits, specifically benefits in kind, is the most uncertain procedure in Nicholson's work and the progressiveness of benefits has almost certainly been overstated. In addition, the Nicholson/C.S.O. studies cannot reflect the full complexity of the total pattern of redistribution since some variables are excluded from their analyses. The estimates we presented in the last chapter were designed to illustrate this fact.

Necessary tax increases are obviously most redistributive if they are confined to modifications in income-tax and surtax and these taxes are also horizontally progressive, especially in the middle income ranges. However, *some* indirect taxes are also minimally regressive or even progressive.[17] Against this background we may note, for example, that the publicized intentions of the Conservative Party; to increase the use made of indirect taxes; to reduce if possible the standard rate of income tax and possibly the magnitude or at least the rate of growth of some welfare expenditures; could have considerable anti-equalitarian potential.

(ii) *The Measurement of Income Redistribution over a period of time*

We may ascribe two meanings to this phrase. The first relates to whether or not there are discernible trends over a period in the amount and direction of income redistribution. The second relates to the infinitely more complex problem of measuring the cumulative and inter-generational effects of redistribution. This latter concept has not attracted any attempts at quantification and since longitudinal studies have not been undertaken we shall not be concerned with this concept in this review of findings. The potential value of longitudinal studies has been emphasized at several points in this and preceeding chapters.

One of the central beliefs which has accompanied the development of welfare policies which we noted in the first chapter, is that our society is becoming, or has recently become, less unequal. This process has been identified as having taken place both through the reduction of pre-redistribution income inequality and through the effects of increasing income redistribution. Social policy is concerned with change in many senses, but has social policy resulted in significant social change in this one respect of reducing income inequality? In asking this we are in fact asking two questions. The first is whether a change of this kind has occurred or not and the second is whether any such change has been consciously pursued or systematically effected through social policies.

The evidence from Nicholson's work is not very conclusive on these points. His data have not always been presented in the same forms and comparisons, even within the years covered by his research, are a little difficult to make. However, the most interesting results are even less dependable because they are those relating to the comparison of pre- and post-war inequality, which involves comparison of Nicholson's findings with those of Barna and Cartter. Allowing for the very great error which may arise from these data, the results nevertheless suggest an interesting conclusion.

Compared with 1937, Nicholson's findings for 1953 suggest that post-redistribution incomes were as unequal in the post-war as in the pre-war period.[18] Moreover there is good reason to assume that the degree of inequality had not changed by 1959.[19] _Therefore, the estimated inequality of final incomes remained constant over a period of twenty years which saw the establishment and growth to some stability, of the 'welfare state'._

The overall changes between 1961 and 1969 amounted to an increase in the regressive effects of taxation, offset by a progressive change in the magnitude of benefits. Nevertheless, it must be noted that any small overall reductions in inequality _between_ income groups that might have occurred during these years were not necessarily accompanied by parallel changes _within_ income groups.

Households containing pensioners or persons receiving National Assistance/Supplementary Benefits, sickness or unemployment benefits for more than a short period of time, may have received varying, but small, degrees of net gain during these years. Within the same income groups households receiving none of these benefits for a significant period of time, suffered regressive increases in national insurance contributions (and some other taxes), which were probably not fully offset by increased public expenditure on benefits in kind. The overall lack of major change in inequality which Nicholson notes, therefore conceals some beneficial and some regressive changes

109

of importance. These smaller changes which have taken place within the overall trends will be examined later.

The most insistent claims for a move towards greater equality were made by those who studied the distribution of pre-redistribution incomes. Nicholson's findings again suggest the absence of any dramatic changes during the whole period. The revised figures derived from Barna's work by Nicholson, suggest a slight decline in the inequality of pre-redistribution incomes; but little reliance can be placed upon the comparison of data from these very different pieces of research. On the basis of Nicholson's own work no significant change in inequality is to be detected between 1953 and 1959.

A small decrease in inequality may have occurred between 1953 and 1957, since an increase in equality occurred between 1957 and 1959, but it would be wise to view these small changes as purely statistical phenomena. It is more difficult to present global assessments of the changes taking place during the sixties, but there is some evidence to suggest an increase in the redistributive effectiveness of social policies. As was the case in the fifties there are conflicting trends at different income levels and for different family sizes, some of which are likely to be real changes and some of which are merely statistical changes which cannot be taken very seriously. The work done by Prest and Stark is interesting in this context. They found a small but steady move towards greater equality in the distribution of per capita income between 1949 and 1963. Their results were based on an equivalence scale which allowed them to weight the per capita distribution of income in households of difference sizes. In the absence of such weighting, however, their data were similar to Nicholson's in failing to indicate a trend in income inequality.[20]

The conclusions to be drawn from Nicholson's work are far more negative than those suggested by other researchers. Nevertheless, concentrating attention on the search for trends over a period of more than twenty years can be misleading. Cartter's research concentrated upon the redistributive processes operating immediately after the second world war. Comparing his results with Barna's he stresses that 'up to 1937 the diminishing degree of inequality of disposable incomes appears to be the result of more equally distributed original incomes, whereas the decline in disposable income inequality from 1937 to 1948 is seen to be almost entirely due to the redistributing effects of direct taxes and transfers'.[21] Measured in terms of Gini coefficients the decline in inequality of disposable income is from twenty-three points in 1937 to sixteen points in 1948.[22] There can be little doubt that this period was one of greater equality compared with the pre-war era. A very approximate diagram of changes in inequality over the period 1937-59 is included below.

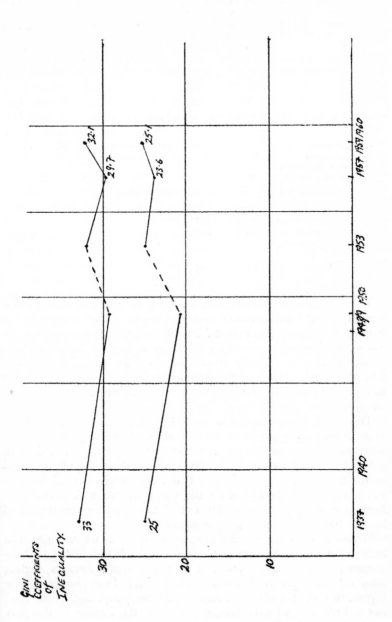

GINI
COEFFICIENTS
OF
INEQUALITY

30

20

10

1937   1940   1944/45   1950   1953   1957   1957/1960

33   32.1
                                 29.7

25   25.1
                                 23.6

(1) The diagram is intended only as a simple and approximate representation of the measured changes in inequality. The Gini coefficients entered on it are those produced by Nicholson. The coefficients used for the other years are calculated on different bases and cannot be directly compared, hence the approximate nature of the diagram. They are presented below for reference.

	1937	1948/9	Reduction in Inequality 1937–48/9
Personal factor Income	27	24	3
Income after taxes and Benefits.	17	14	3
Reduction in inequality within each year.	10	10	

Source: Cartter op. cit. Tables 32 and 33, pp. 74–5.

	1937		1957	1959
Producers' income	33	Pre-redistribution Income	29·7	32·1
Consumers' income	25	Post-redistribution Income	23·6	25·1
Reduction in inequality within each year	8		6·1	7

Source: Nicholson, J. L., op. cit., p. 61 and Table VIII, p. 45.

	1953	1959
Pre-redistribution Income	33.5	33.7
'Disposable Income'	24·9	25·0
Reduction in inequality within each year.	8.6	8.7

Source: Nicholson, J. L., Table X, P. 46.

The definitions of income vary between the research workers and the only direct comparisons of data that can be made are those in the footnote to the diagram. Personal Factor Incomes in particular are not exactly similar to pre-redistribution income as used by Nicholson. Disposable income in each case refers to original incomes after the addition of direct benefits and the subtraction of direct taxes. Disposable incomes are therefore more equal than are final or post-redistribution incomes.

The broad changes are clear enough, but the findings are subject to great error. The period of the second world war was characterized by a move towards greater inequality which partly resulted from changes in initial income inequality. This trend was rapidly reversed in the late forties and early fifties and the distribution of incomes was as unequal at the end of the fifties as it was in 1937. Throughout these years the redistributive effect of all taxes and benefits (allocated by the studies) was remarkably constant.

Within these very general and speculative trends we can note in a little more detail some of the micro-changes which seem to have occurred during recent years. The recent move towards slightly more estimated progression has resulted mainly from changes in the expenditure on benefits, but higher income groups appear to have lost a little ground over recent years and the change is therefore partly a vertical shift.

This increased progressiveness may in theory reflect an improvement in the position of middle income earners rather than low income earners, or in the position of one type of family and it is important to identify the precise pattern of redistributive change. In fact the improvement is concentrated upon the lowest income groups and families remaining in these very low income categories over the period would have benefited to a noticeable degree.[23] Although small the identified changes appear to be of the classical and much desired kind; vertical redistribution in favour of the poorest households. The official commentary also suggests that the middle and lower middle income groups were not noticeable beneficiaries, the change being exclusively to the benefit of the poorest. But it must be noted that these very low income groups may be comprised almost solely of pensioner households and other households without children.[24] The question to be asked is whether low income families *with children* have benefitted from changes in the redistributive processes between 1961 and 1967.

In practice pensioner households are concentrated in the very lowest income bracket, but the main types of households in other income groups benefiting from this shift in redistribution did not contain children. Households with children were to be found, in 1967, almost exclusively in income brackets above those which the increase in redistribution had affected.[25] These figures therefore confirm what one might have expected from the policies of the period. Families with children benefited little, if at all, from any move towards greater progression. However, those few families with children to be found in the very lowest income ranges, may have benefited from significant improvements.

In summary, a *small amount of increased vertical redistribution was concentrated on the lowest income households, but largely failed to assist poor families with children for this very reason.* The extent to which families with children benefited from increased horizontal redistribution (within income groups) is impossible to ascertain. Only one indication of this possibility is worth mentioning; it modifies what we have just said about vertical redistribution. Families with four children gained considerably relative to other family types between 1961 and 1967 and this one type of family appears, therefore, to have benefited from a horizontal shift in the distribution of taxation and benefits.[26]

A final, paradoxical change may be mentioned which indicates the complexity of the processes we are considering and the value of research as sophisticated as the Nicholson/C.S.O. studies. The very family type we have just mentioned, also gained least from the rise in *original* incomes. Their original incomes rose by an average of 11%

113

between 1961 and 1964 and 26% between 1961 and 1967, compared with an overall average for all family types of 18% and 42% in the same two periods of time. One person households experienced a rise of 43% and 61% over these time spans. The increased horizontal redistribution benefiting families with four children was merely offsetting a slow rate of increase in their original incomes.

Families with four children were concentrated entirely within the income ranges £800—£2,000 in the sample. The number of respondents is small and great care is required in interpreting the results. However, assuming the data to be a reasonable representation of actual trends, it may be that the findings for this family type reflect a more widespread tendency for lower initial incomes to increase relatively slowly. In the absence of increased redistribution such households would certainly have suffered a very considerable relative fall in their standards of living. Such anomalies are the first fruits of, and the impetus for more, detailed research. Future research should be directly related to changes in social policy and should differentiate, where possible, between the varying experiences of families in substantially different circumstances and in different regions of the country.

Social Policy and the Redistribution of Income

We are now in a position to answer the questions we asked earlier about the role of social policy in producing greater income (in-)equality. To judge from Nicholson's findings the answer must be largely a negative one, for neither pre- nor post-redistribution incomes have become substantially more equal since before the war. At any one time welfare policies seem to be effective in reducing inequality; but the major post-war policy changes, which have been so widely assumed to be beneficent and equalitarian, have made no difference to estimates of inequality.

It must be borne in mind that the process of estimation may have concealed changes that have taken place. Equally, the degree of inequality and extent of redistribution may have been incorrectly quantified in view of the enormous methodological problems that we have outlined. Such errors may also have grown or diminished in importance over time and there is no way of ascertaining which of these factors have to be allowed for in interpreting the data.

Some factors (such as non-monetary income, for example) which may result in error when excluded, would most probably make initial incomes appear more unequal if they were included. Moreover those items of income which have been neglected are, to say the least, as likely to have increased inequality over time as to have reduced it. We may equally assume that errors in estimating benefits are not likely to have concealed substantial increases in progressive redistribution and the basic distribution of benefits is almost certainly too optimistically progressive, as we have argued. The judgment expressed by Professor Abel-Smith in the late fifties that 'the main effect of the post war development of the social services, the creation of the "Welfare State", has been to provide free social services to the middle classes' appears to be as relevant now as it was then.[27] The post-war extension of social welfare has not yet produced major changes in inequality which benefit the poor, partly because a large number of these post-war welfare programmes were specifically designed 'to afford roughly equal per capita, rather than strictly redistributive benefits.'[28] On the other hand, these social policy changes do not appear to have reduced the effectiveness of the redistributive processes existing before and during the war period.

This last impression requires some modification, for as Cartter noted, while the total amount of redistribution increased considerably over the war period, (an estimated 8.8% of National Income was redistributed in 1937, 13.1% in 1948/9), the rate of redistribution per pound of taxation declined sharply. In 1937 40.6% of taxation was redistributive in effect, in 1948/9 this had fallen to 31.8%.[29] It seems that the introduction and development of the 'welfare state' took place during a potentially anti-redistributive period. The growth in the sum total of taxation and particularly the considerable changes in the levels of income tax and surtax, were crucial to the maintenance of post-war redistribution at a level equal to or above that of the pre-war era.

This is not to suggest that post-war social policy has been of little relevance to the attempt to bring under conscious control the social structure, values and processes of change to be found in our society. Social policy may be said to encompass many more objectives than that of redistribution. Yet redistribution and the continuing amelioration of inequality is one of the most obvious and widely accepted criteria against which social policy may be judged and one of the very few against which some holistic, quantitative assessment of performance may be obtained. It is particularly important to accept and utilize this negative judgment on the spate of post-war policy changes in future planning, precisely because redistribution is a central and quantifiable criterion. We are already witnessing an adjustment to the shortcomings of past planning in discussions and research upon non-utilization of welfare services, the development of positively discriminatory programmes, and the growth of interest in community development projects.

A wider problem is to be located in the nature of social policy and social planning itself. The 'objectives' of social policy have been mentioned and despite its convenience this shorthand notation is misleading. Social policy cannot be discussed in terms of objectives in this manner, for objectives are the possessions of individuals or corporate entities, but who or what 'possesses' the objectives of social policy? Social policy is a useful concept which, in our society at least, is not embodied within a unitary planning process or organization. By way of comparison, even such a broad category of activities as 'economic planning' can be seen to exhibit far more continuity and coherence, if only in its organization and not its substantive manifestations.

For precisely this reason we may doubt whether an 'objective' as broad as that of fostering income redistribution could be achieved as the end result of social policy activities. Not only are specific social policies developed and urged upon authorities for many reasons other than that of enhancing redistribution, (some of them being exclusive of and others contradictory to this equalitarian process); but social policies are also promulgated and enacted by groups which operate upon or espouse basic orientations which exclude redistribution as a central focus of these policies. Major areas of policy making are therefore unlikely, even in theory, to be progressively redistributive.

We have noted a distinction made at a high level of generality by Professor Titmuss, between three such areas. Of these the least redistributively oriented in theory, occupational welfare, has not been evaluated by the techniques referred to in this book.[30] Of the other two systems, only certain features of both fiscal and social welfare have been quantified in measures of redistribution. We have argued that one desirable innovation would be studies of the distribution and value to households of different forms of recognition accorded to similar social needs. The distribution of all welfare benefits is far more unequal and regressive than is the estimated distribution of taxes net of allocated benefits. We have previously illustrated this point by making reference to the total range of housing and educational subsidies compared with those that are allocated in Nicholson's study. Considering only the more redistributive fiscal and social welfare systems, on the basis of a favourable selection of all welfare policies and during a period widely acclaimed as egalitarian; we have seen that our society has remained fairly consistently unequal.

To effect increased overall redistribution in the future would require far more detailed and co-ordinated social planning, in circumstances which made more unitary the values and objectives of different sectors of the social policy making systems. Detailed evidence is required for sophisticated planning and the emergence of such evidence in our field of interest is what we have discussed in this

116

paper. The capacity and opportunity for such planning has also improved, but the circumstances necessary for the pursuit of increased overall redistribution can hardly be said to exist.

Two limiting factors of importance may be noted. The first is that of economic policy and the continuing strain on the economy. The Labour Party prior to and during the 1964 General Election offered an alternative to the Conservative Government's record of public welfare expenditure. This alternative, of increased public expenditure financed from a more rapid growth of Gross National Product, has not been the panacea that was sought. Despite the slow rate of growth, public expenditure on the social services increased during the late sixties. This process cannot continue for long for socio-political reasons. These constitute the second limitation upon income redistribution.

Indeed one may question how far economic difficulties will be the most crucial determinant of the growth of public welfare expenditure in the future. The impact of 'affluence' (particularly improvements in the real incomes of middle and lower middle income groups) on political life and policy making, may be of greater importance. If social class based support for the Labour Party as 'champion' of a holistic commitment to the 'welfare state' declines, any move towards greater public expenditure and income redistribution would seem to be dependent upon the power of relevant interest groups to secure adequate priority for these objectives. To a certain extent the importance of such interest groups has always been considerable, but they have operated *within* the context of this holistic response to the rather ill defined, but vaguely redistributive, complex of social policy objectives.

The Child Poverty Action Group is a clear example of one such interest group with considerable relevance for the topic of income redistribution. But the attempt to indicate and enforce upon the Labour Government the objective which the party has traditionally espoused, (and this has been an important feature of the poverty debate) underlines our point that at present such interest groups operate within a largely social class based commitment to enhancing the 'welfare state'.

Dahrendorf is but one observer who has noted the present, and predicted the increasing future, importance of non-class aligned interest groups as the basis for social and political conflict. If this development is further substantiated in the future, the nature and loci of pressures for social policy change will themselves undergo radical change.[31] The level of income redistribution does not vary directly with the level of public expenditure. The former could be maintained or increased without increasing the latter. Indeed a reduction in social welfare expenditure could be accompanied, in theory at least, by an increased rate of income redistribution to lower income groups. Nevertheless, we would argue that there will be decreasing support for substantial increases in public expenditure in the future. Changes in the socio-political structure of our society consequent upon 'affluence' will also make egalitarian 'selective' social policies unrealistic. A rigorous pursuit of income redistribution within existing levels of expenditure would exacerbate the 'contributor'—'beneficiary' dichotomy. People would tend to become increasingly aware of their role as 'contributors' if they felt the poor were the sole 'beneficiaries' of the social services. It, therefore, seems unlikely that substantial increases in income redistribution will receive political support in the forseeable future. We may be confined to making progress towards greater equality, if at all, by further piecemeal redistributive improvements designed to assist particular geographical areas, groups of dependents, and types of social need.

However, even egalitarian reforms of limited scope are most likely to be effective if pursued against a background of increasingly sophisticated knowledge of existing patterns of inequality and income redistribution. Large scale measures of inequality and redistribution do not depend for their usefulness upon the possibility of making equally comprehensive changes in social policy.

From the evidence made available through the considerable achievements of Nicholson and the C.S.O., it should at least be apparent that there is reason to depart from Professor Galbraith's priorities for social policy which we mentioned in chapter one. We may legitimately emphasize the continued need to *both* increase public expenditure and increase levels of income redistribution. Mistrust of public expenditure may well be engendered by fears of its redistributive function, but redistribution can hardly be said to have been so radical in the recent past as to make its maintenance and enhancement unnecessary in the future.

NOTES

1. See the Ministry of Social Security Act 1966 and also the first Annual Report of the Ministry of Social Security.
2. Davies B., and Reddin, M., in New Society, 11th May 1967. Davies, B., and Williamson, V., in Social and Economic Administration, March 1968. Mike Reddin In Townsend P. 'Social Services for all', Fabian Society, 1968.
3. Peacock, A. and Shannon, R., op. cit., p. 45.
4. They produce an outline of this budget in Table II, ibid., p. 35.
5. Barna's alternative assumptions were discussed in Chapter 4.
6. Peacock, A. and Shannon, R., op. cit., p. 46.
7. The Gini coefficient is a useful means of representing overall changes in income inequality, but it is a crude index and this must be borne in mind. Gini coefficients indicating a reduction of inequality do not indicate the source of change. A reduced concentration of income among the wealthy in favour of middle income families, a loss of income among middle income families to the benefit of poorer families, or even a loss of income by the poor and the rich in favour of the middle income earners, could all appear as a reduction of income inequality. The Gini coefficient does not help us distinguish these different phenomena. Equally, complex changes in inequality could cancel each other out and would not be reflected

in the Gini coefficient. Despite these defects the coefficient provides a very economic means of summarizing large amounts of data.

8. Nicholson, op. cit., Table VIII, p. 45.

9. Ibid., Table X, p. 46.

10. Economic Trends, February 1969, especially Table 3(·). Changes during this period are considered in some detail later.

11. In the most recent analysis, useful additional data have been made available by including pensioner households, and distinguishing between households with and without retired heads of households.

12. Economic Trends, February 1969.

13. Nicholson, op. cit., p. 19.

14. Ibid., p. VIII.

15. Economic Trends, February 1969, Table 3(IV).

16. These broad trends are confirmed for the period 1961–68 in Economic Trends, February 1970, pp. XXIV–V.

17. The effects of different types of indirect tax are mentioned in several of the issues of Economic Trends referred to, most usefully in Feb. 1969. The most clearly regressive indirect taxes are local rates and tobacco duties. Duty on alcoholic drinks is progressive in the case of wines and spirits and regressive in the case of beer. Indirect taxes on intermediate products are estimated to be mildly regressive, while both local rates and duty on alcholic drinks are somewhat progressive horizontally.

18. Nicholson, op. cit., p. 60.

19. Ibid., Table X, p. 46. The overall change between 1959 and 1968 is also very small.

20. Prest, A. R., and Stark, T. L., 'Some Aspects of Income Distribution in the U.K. since World War II'. The Manchester School, Vol. 25, No. 3, September 1967, Tables 1 and 2, pp. 226–7.

21. Cartter, op. cit., p. 76.

22. Ibid., taken from Table 33, p. 75.

23. Economic Trends, February 1969, p. XVIII and T.3(i).

24. Ibid., useful additional information has been made available for recent years on pensioner households and other households containing pensioners.

25. Economic Trends, February 1969, Table 3(i) and Table 7.

26. Ibid., Table 4.

27. Abel-Smith, B., in 'Conviction', ed. MacKenzie, N., London, MacGibbon & Kee, 1959, p. 57.

28. Cartter, op. cit., p. 66.

29. Ibid., p. 66.

30. Indeed far too little social policy writing has been concerned with the field of occupational welfare in any respect.

31. Dahrendorf, R., 'Conflict after Class', Longmans, University of Essex, Noel Buxton, Lecture 1967.

The studies of redistribution undertaken by Barna and Cartter.

The contribution to the study of redistribution made by the Family Expenditure Survey and the Nicholson/C.S.O. analyses can only be appreciated if the early studies by Barna and Cartter are studied. The problems they faced are briefly summarized below.

As we noted in the main text their data on the distribution of initial incomes relied upon official administrative statistics. A detailed criticism of the initial income distribution will not be undertaken, but it should be noted that information on income was therefore incomplete in so far as income tax returns fail to gather sufficient data on non-monetary forms of remuneration. Similarly the absence of a capital-income unit resulted in an inadequate representation of the distribution of net annual changes in purchasing power. Income statistics available from the operation of the Board of Inland Revenue relate to tax units and not biological or economic family units, this presented considerable difficulties for Barna and Cartter. Professor Titmuss discussed these problems and those of tax evasion and avoidance in great detail.[1] The means by which taxation and benefits were allocated to the initial income distribution, by Barna and Cartter, in order to gain a measure of redistribution, will now be discussed.

(i) Barna's Study

Due to the absence of information on the composition of actual households and on their corresponding household income and expenditure, both Barna and Cartter were restricted to a calculation of the distribution of total population by income range, rather than the distribution of actual households or income units. Barna estimated that the average number of persons per 'income tax family' was 2.57 over the whole income range above the statutory tax exemption limit. He, therefore, proceeded to multiply the number of income tax returns in each income range by this figure, to provide an estimate of population distribution by income.

This device immediately discounts the correlation between income and family size. It also depends on an assumption that Professor Titmuss has shown to be unsatisfactory, namely, that each income tax return represents an 'income tax family', of a man, his wife (if married) and any dependent children (under 16 years of age or in full time education).[2] Separate returns by wives and on behalf of children disrupt this basic concept. The crucial point for our purpose is that the process of submitting separate tax returns for individual members of the family, is not randomly distributed among income ranges. Barna probably over estimated the number of persons in the highest income groups in this instance as well as doing so by assuming a lack of correlation between income and family size. The problem is that by the fragmentation of household income through the submission of separate returns, each of the somewhat smaller portions of it are allocated to lower income ranges than that which the total household income would have warranted. If separate returns were not successfully 'married' Barna's figures would be an underestimate of the extent of inequality. These forces were probably very much less intrusive in Barna's 1937 study than they were post the Second World War. These sources of error nevertheless remain as an important ground for entertaining reservations with respect to the final results.

Barna was forced by the absence of data on family or household incomes to estimate the incidence of taxation using the Board of Inland Revenue data as a basis. This procedure need not be described in detail, but an example of its unsatisfactory nature can be given. To compute the impact of income tax, he deducted the appropriate tax allowances from the income data available from tax returns. This clearly involved an estimate of the distribution of children by income range, for which data from social surveys was used.[3] Regardless of the merits of the data, the application of them to tax return figures again neglected the fact that these returns were not necessarily representative of the number of families per income range. To obtain an estimate of taxable income for each income range he therefore had to use a procedure which gave rise to the possibility of considerable errors in the deduction of tax allowances for wives and children. Barna's method of estimating the incidence of income tax is open to much criticism of this kind.

Indirect taxes on expenditure were allocated mainly on the basis of arbitrary assumptions since no analysis of expenditure on alcohol, tobacco and most other consumption goods, was available. Taxes on food were based on the estimates of expenditure on such goods by different income groups, that independent research findings made possible.[4] However, Barna's assumed distribution of persons by income was utilized in arriving at an expenditure-per-person estimate. In view of the unsatisfactory nature of this population estimate, error may be suspected, probably tending to overstate the indirect taxation on upper incomes.

Rents, being the only form of housing expenditure on which data were available, were assumed representatively of all housing costs and were generalized to the total population. It was on this basis that local rates were deducted from the different income ranges. Most revealing perhaps of the difficulties facing Barna in making the complex integration of private research and public administrative data, are the estimates of clothing expenditure. Allocating this item by reference to lower and middle income expenditure patterns, resulted in a total initial allocated sum 20% below the sum spent nationally on clothing.[5]

Enough has been said to indicate the nature of the possible errors and, by implication, of the kind of data needed for a more satisfactory study. It would not be helpful to describe the process of allocation in further details, for no estimation of the possible direction or magnitude of bias in the final results is possible. Comparison with Nicholson's methodology can be made, however, on the basis of the foregoing brief comments. To correct any impression conveyed of such errors uniformly producing a more egalitarian result than the actual situation warranted, it should be noted that the allocation of benefits by reference to the estimated population distribution may have inflated the imputed benefits to the upper income groups. This was most possible with respect to Public Health expenditures. On the other hand public expenditure on education was not imputed to income groups presumed to be purchasing education privately; this is contrary to Nicholson's procedure.

The allocation of public expenditure on education was achieved by first assuming that all families with incomes over £400 failed to use public elementary schools. This assumption was based on the fact that 7.3 per cent of the population (of school aged children) did not utlize this public elementary education and that the same proportion of the population were found to have incomes in excess of £400.[6] A number of factors could invalidate this assumption not least the fact that the top 7.3% of income units need not have included 7.3% of the school age child population. However, in view of the paucity of data on which Barna could proceed, this may be accepted as an initial assumption productive of a relatively small amount of bias. The expenditure on ex-elementary school pupils in secondary schools, who were over the statutory minimum school leaving age, was apportioned by reference to the chance of such children coming from families within given income ranges.[7] This element of expenditure was, therefore, adjusted to reflect the greater educational benefit accruing to the middle income groups. The largest item of expenditure, however, that relating to children below the statutory teminal age, was allocated by reference to the number of persons in each income range below £400 and it did not reflect the differential benefits gained from elementary and secondary education by different income groups. Despite the lack of information on which to make an adjustment an arbitrary differential allocation could have been attempted, whereas in fact the doubtful validity of the procedure was not indicated by Barna.

In contrast to Cartter it should be borne in mind that both Barna and Nicholson allocate local authority taxation and expenditure. Cartter, that is to say, excluded all public expenditures by local authorities that were financed by local taxation.

Finally before proceeding from this rapid outline of Barna's methodology, it is interesting to note that some benefits emanating from Friendly Societies and Trade Unions, were allocated by him. This is the only deviation from the policy of considering only State financed welfare services to be found in the three studies of resdistribution. In view of this very restricted attention to extra-State recognition of social need, Barna cannot be said to offer a more acceptable definition of re-distribution or social service for our purpose than either of the other researchers, for other occupational and all fiscal benefits were excluded.

Barna arrived at an approximate estimation of the extent of re-distribution through public finance as a result of his study. To be more precise he provided alternative estimates based on different assumptions as to the allocation of indivisible benefits and public income.[8] He concluded that 'whatever assumption is made, the direction of the re-distribution of incomes was from the rich to the poor and its amount, best put at £200–250 mn., was substantial'.[9] This conclusion was certainly tempered with important reservations, for as he stressed 'the final distribution of incomes, after allowing for the effects of redistribution, was still far from being equal.'[10] This fact, in conjunction with the observation that 'want, in the crudest sense of the word, could have been abolished by a further redistribution of income of relatively modest porportion', lead him to assert that 'social justice demands redistribution of incomes greater than that recorded.[11]

Simultaneously he considered it to be 'broadly true that the amount redistributed was a progressive proportion of income and therefore, the system of public finance as a whole was satisfactory'.[12] His methodology as we have briefly indicated, does not permit complete confidence in this judgment on the efficacy of income redistribution process in 1937. The results of Cartter's work suggest that the social welfare and taxation policies of the war and immediate post-war years, had substantially enhanced these redistributive processes. Cartter's methodological problems may also be reviewed very briefly.

(ii) Cartter's Study

Although the study Cartter undertook of the redistribution process in 1948/49 was based on very similar data to that of Barna's in 1937, one or two of the assumptions which he had to make where data were lacking, can be profitably examined since the post war policies in welfare provision differed in philosophy from those of 1937. As Cartter noted the most distinguishing feature of the new policies was their universality, which made it 'more appropriate to assume an equal per capita distribution for many programmes' than was the case prior to the war.[13] In the earlier period some assumptions about the beneficiaries of State financed welfare services were possible, on logical if not empirical grounds, in terms of the more narrowly defined social groups which the services were legislated to benefit. In view of the post-war change in social welfare philosophy it is particularly crucial that Cartter's allocation of benefits should have reflected accurately the impact of these policies rather than quantify the expectations which the more egalitarian philosophy engendered. In practice much of the allocation of benefits rested upon little or no empirical evidence on patterns of usage of the services concerned; this evidence was not available. The year chosen presented the complex problem of distinguishing between the benefits and taxes accruing from the last months of the earlier services and the first months of the emergent ones. At best it is not possible to determine which pattern of social services had the major impact in producing the level of redistribution that Cartter measured. More seriously the new section of the population being phased into the insurance schemes were making contributions not offset by their full benefit rights, thus of necessity producing an illusion of greater equality after redistribution than would be expected once the phasing-in had been completed.

As an example of the assumptions which Cartter found necessary; in allocating old age and retirement pensions he 'assumed that the number of elderly persons as a percentage of total persons in each income group varied inversely with size of income, over the three lowest income groups.[14] The allocation of distributed benefit to the lowest income groups is not disputed but the allocation within these groups based on the assumption quoted above may have provided a spuriously egalitarian effect. The allocation of *all* pension benefits to the *three lowest income groups*, though acceptable in terms of the 1948/49 situation, illustrates the hiatus between valid assumptions for that year and the equal per capita distribution which he noted as the long term aim of the universality principle.

This is primarily a criticism of the year Cartter chose to study, of the exclusive reliance upon a single year over which to measure the effects of redistribution, and of the confident assertion of results based on admittedly arbitrary assumptions in the absence of reliable data. In additional several of the assumptions used in imputing benefits to income groups may be mentioned briefly to indicate the grave deficiency of the information available on consumer use of services with which Cartter had to contend. Educational expenditure was distributed between income groups on the belief that in those income groups below £750 all children attended maintained schools. No attempt was made to differentiate between the benefits accruing from different forms (primary, secondary grammar, secondary modern) of schooling received. Benefits were not considered to accrue to children in public and other non State aided schools. All children in the income group above £1,000 were assumed to be in public (independent) schools and 45% of those in the £750–£1,000 range were not allocated benefit for the same reason. Bias due to the lack of information on the receipt of privately financed education, significant though it may be, is marginal compared with the inability to differentiate between the types of State education received. The lack of detailed information, rather than Cartter's assumptions, was probably more damaging in this instance.

The expenditure on health services was imputed to all persons assumed to be registered, that is all those in the income group below £1,000. Above this figure the proportion of persons registered in each income range was taken to be in inverse ratio with income, thus only 25% of persons in the two highest income groups were estimated to be registered. As with education, however, the almost total lack of information on the use made of services is the most crucial difficulty. Cartter estimated on the basis of various tangential studies that the elderly needed double the attention required by the average adult (15–65 years) and that the child under 15 years of age, seven times this amount.[15] It was on this basis and by reference to the estimated distribution of persons of each age group between income ranges, that National Health Service benefits were imputed.

In addition to the crucial decisions about the taxes and benefits to be included in the study, both these researchers faced a number of problems which seriously weakened their studies. The basic data available to them on the distribution of incomes were deficient and the distribution of incomes between families had to be estimated, much error may have arisen during this process. The incidence of taxation and welfare benefits had also to be estimated using a variety of data and assumptions. The resulting findings must therefore be used with great care.

NOTES

1. Titmuss, R. M., (1962), op. cit.
2. Barna makes the assumption that this is the statutory definition employed by the Board of Inland Revenue. Barna, T., op. cit., p. 63.
3. Ibid., p. 89.
4. Ibid., p. 150.
5. Ibid., p. 156.
6. Ibid., p. 204.
7. Ibid., p. 205.
8. Public income is defined as 'the income of the government from property and trading, together with the investment income of public charaties'. Ibid. p. 16.
9. Ibid., p. 233.
10. Ibid., p. 233.
11. Ibid., p. 234.
12. Ibid., p. 233.
13. Chartter, A. M., op. cit., p. 206.
14. Ibid., p. 209.
15. The method of allocation is essentially an arbitary one due to the very limited information available to Cartter on differential needs and benefits gained from the health services. Ibid., pp. 223–4.

Adjustments for non-response 1957–62.

In 1957 the method of adjustment used was to compare the distribution of different types of income tax unit by income range in the Board of Inland Revenue data with the corresponding tax units contained within the households comprising the Family Expenditure Survey. The weights to be applied to the data for households in each cell, were calculated by minimizing the difference between the distribution of tax units in the sample and the Board's estimates.[1] This method was applied to only some classifications of the 1957 data, for other tables a more sophisticated correction was used.[2]

The latter was based on a process of subtracting the distribution of income tax units contained in the sample of households from that of the Board of Inland Revenue's distribution leaving the distribution of tax units in 'missing' households. The means of adjusting the sample of households to absorb these missing units is detailed in an appendix to Nicholson's book. What is of importance for our purposes is a consideration of the values of these methods in terms of the measures of inequality which are calculated from the adjusted data. As Nicholson mentions, the difficulty with the first is that the distribution of households by type in the income groups is not necessarily reliable in the adjusted figures. He therefore considers the second to be more satisfactory, however, as in both cases Inland Revenue data on the distribution of income units were used the possibility of avoiding deficiencies in this data source is limited.

In comparison with this relatively minor criticism the sophistication of the adjustments must not be allowed to obscure the serious weakness of the basic sample itself. Regardless of how well the adjustment is made, this can only reweight the data provided by families actually co-operating in the survey. Where in a fine analysis the number of respondents in each cell (i.e. of the household composition/income range classification) are extremely low, the recorded details cannot be confidently taken as representative of that group of households in the population generally. This difficulty is most marked in the top income groups where as few as one or two families of a given size provide data for a critical income range. In view of the poor coverage of the upper income ranges, the sample as a whole, even after adjustment, cannot be viewed as if it were representative of the total population. Or more precisely the adjusted sampled may be representative of the population, but the data are far less likely to be so.

The adjustment applied in 1959 differed from those already noted and while more appropriate for correcting the effects of non-response on the distribution of households by household composition, it does not give greater confidence that the bias in the distribution by income range is neutralized. Households not willing to participate fully were requested to provide more limited information on several topics, household composition, type of dwelling, housing costs and ownership of durable goods. They thus had four alternate sets of limited information which they could provide, household composition only, this and details on the type of dwelling occupied, the previous two plus housing costs, adding durable goods data for the fourth category. By allocating the households giving the minimum amount of information, that is to say that on household composition only, to a type of dwelling on the basis of the proportions of households of the same household composition in each of the three types of dwelling, in the remaining categories of limited response, Nicholson was able to eliminate the group provided least information.[3] By this process all the limited response households were allocated a type of dwelling, a level of housing costs and a level of durable goods ownership.

The adjustment assumes that the households willing to give information on their household composition only, were distributed among dwelling types by household type in the same way as were all households giving only limited information. Even at this first stage it can be seen that households giving the least information may differ systematically with respect to dwelling type, from all other households, the assumption may therefore be invalid. At the last stage it is equally clear that households willing to co-operate fully and all those providing limited information only, may differ in terms of income, holding all other factors constant, yet this is assumed not to be the case. Even if no systematic bias is present with respect to income itself, errors in the preceding stages may result in incorrect allocation to income ranges. The adjustment may not have eliminated the bias of the sample and the small cell numbers will have endangered the representativeness of data collected, as has been indicated previously.

In addition to the problem of non response among high and low income groups, families with a large number of children (four or more) or of unusual composition are also represented by very few respondents in the samples. In 1959 the proportion of four children households with respect to the population of households generally is less likely to be inaccurate in the adjusted sample than in previous years, but the distribution by income range may still be in error. Families with more than four children are not analysed separately. This is mentioned because if we were to estimate the inequality of income per capita, the larger family assumes as great an importance, in terms of gaining an adequate representation of this section of the population and an accurate distribution of the household size by income range, as does the representation of the highest income group given the present method of measuring the inequality of income distribution.

Adjustments for non-response have not been made since 1962.

NOTES

1. Nicholson, J. L., op. cit., p. 63.
2. Ibid., pp. 63–4.
3. Ibid., 64–5.